For:

Robert

my friend, mentor and
opener of the Dream Gates.

My Gratitude to you extends
all time.

Love,
Sn
2011

THE POWER OF DREAMS

The Power of

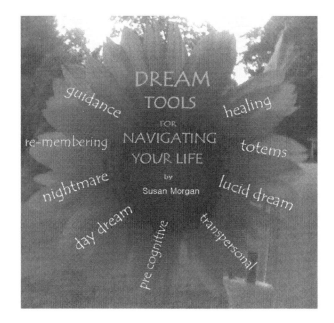

DREAM
TOOLS
FOR
NAVIGATING
YOUR LIFE
by
Susan Morgan

guidance
healing
re-membering
totems
nightmare
lucid dream
day dream
pre cognitive
transpersonal

DREAMS

THE POWER OF DREAMS

Dream Tools for Navigating Your Life

SUSAN L. MORGAN

ISBN-13: 978-1463500450

First Printing, 2011

This book is lovingly dedicated to

my children;

James, Charlotte and Gabriel.

May you always have your Dreams

to navigate your life;

your true North Star.

THE POWER OF DREAMS

Table of Contents

Introduction

Working for more than a decade in the trans-formational art of dream interpretation, I have found that most people do not know the value of remembering their dreams. Yet you *can* learn how to remember and understand them, and in your understanding receive some of the greatest gifts of your life. Though there is already a ple-thora of dream books, fresh words are always good, and I offer you mine.

Every one reading this book can learn how to read their dreams and develop a language with their Soul. Dreams are often poetic, usually in metaphor, and connected like a gossamer thread directly to our Soul. *The only mystery is the mystery that you are to yourself.*

Do you know what a purple alien means to *you* if you dreamed one last night? How about a three ton elephant?

Don't run to the nearest dream dictionary, unless that is to throw it out. Stop. Spend a few minutes with your immense prolific self, and let the image simmer in your mind a moment or two. You have a memory thread somewhere in you of this image or your inner self would have pulled another image for you to relate this dream to. Your thoughts and feelings for example, of the purple alien, are linked to your thoughts and feeling in this dream you had last night.

And yet, this is *not* an intellectual exercise.

If you are having trouble rounding up the purple alien meaning in your memory bank (maybe the bank is closed), you will find it easier if you look for the feeling connected to it. Start with wide and sweeping associations before narrowing your search.

Think random connectedness and you will enter the territory of the dreamworld faster.

Dreaming is Not Elitist

Dreaming is not an elitist activity. You do not need an expensive education to understand what your heart knows every night. Do you think the Andaman tribe that climbed their mountain to avoid the oncoming tsunami in 2004, did so after they read and studied about it? (The same tsunami that claimed the lives of nearly a quarter million people) They knew it from their dreams, and their ability to read the signs of nature.

We can all access the guidance we need from our dreams. We can be assured of this, in much the same way we are gifted by our very birth on this Earth; with water, air, sun, the beat of our heart and so much more. God does not want to make things any more difficult than necessary for us. I am convinced of this. It is we that add the distractions that make our lives and the paths we travel harder than they need to be.

A flower blooms effortlessly every morning, its' connection with the divine unimpeded.

May I stand next to my door to the Divine, and not block it. May I have an unbroken cord to the Sacred.

Knowledge can be accessed by more than one means. Dreams are our golden cord to All That Is, making them precious indeed.

During the final edit of this book and I had this dream:

Healing Dream Centers

I meet a woman who shares a story with me about how she received needed clarity in her life; she went to a 'special wing' of a 'special hospital' that ran a program called: *The Trans-personal Healing Art of Dreamwork*. I am both shocked and thrilled by the knowledge that there is a formal, mainstream establishment whose approach to dreamwork is like mine! I am told by the 'Narrator' (oh dear guardian of mine) in my dream that I too can create a place like this. The model for it is already done. *EOD* (end of dream)

Upon waking I decide to hold this dream as a compass point for the creation of dream centers like this, so that we can all have access to the nurturing help of our dreams. The time is over-ripe for our mainstream culture to recognize the power we can access every night for our own well being, as well as the well being of our Earth.

My hope for you is that by reading these stories of how dreams have impacted my life, as well as others, you might consider your dreams in a new light. The exercises at the end of many of the chapters offer a way to further help you develop a working relationship with your dreams. By the time you finish this book, you will be well on your way to becoming a Conscious Dreamer. Dream On!

Acknowledgements

I would like to thank and honor those who helped make this book possible. The first thanks goes to my son Gabriel, whose encouragement is endless and who holds the faith that I have something worthwhile to say and that people will benefit from it. Times too numerous to count, he reminds me to put aside the busyness of life and just sit and write!

I also have a deep debt of gratitude to my friend and mentor Robert Moss, whose dedication to Dreams and the Dreamworld is unsurpassed. He is an inspiration to thousands.

I also want to thank my father Paul Meals, who always asked me when I was a little girl what my dreams were. He also taught me to think large and remember we are not alone in the Universe.

And lastly, thanks go to my Guardians and Guides in the Dreamworld, who told me years ago that though I am not perfect; *my heart is good enough*, and they need my help. I would add that we all have hearts that are good enough and all our help is needed.

Much Love to All,

Susan Morgan

Chapter One

MY STORY

(or a part thereof)

I have been dreaming as far back as I can remember. I have indulged myself in day dreaming more than most. All of my creative ventures ranging from painting, gardening, home decorating, the naming of my children etc., have been incubated in my day dreaming world. And I know I am not alone in this way of working creatively.

For the better part of my life, my technique has been to lie down for about twenty minutes and drift in between sleep and wakefulness, hovering in the numinous space between the two. I start with my intention of what I am looking for, and without exception, I get clear images. I have often received detailed information like when I recently took a 'nap' to try to figure out how to build an island in my kitchen. My request included: with little or no money. I was shown the final result first (beautiful!) and then detailed instructions on how to build it. I had no prior building expertise, and I have to say I am quite proud of the result and all for under $100! (building on a budget is another book for another day)

Daydreams

When I was young I would drift into a day-dream, while in school, to break the monotony of sitting stationary for hours.

I would stare out the window and letting my imagination drift, take a break from the reality of my classroom. The first day of school in fifth grade I was horrified to see that my new class-room had a view of a brick wall, and nothing else. (an old building that modern zoning laws would never have approved) My seat was in the back corner, next to the windows and bricks. Within the first month of Autumn I was delighted to find that the brick held no barrier to my imagi-nation.

I wonder now if we are doing our children a disservice when we are overly concerned when they are not paying attention. In reality they are paying attention, just not to what we want them to focus on. We even medicate them some-times over this 'problem.' Our day dreams and the active imagination that goes along with it are, I believe, critical to our happiness; certainly as a key antidote to stress. We connect with another realm in imagination. From the pers-pective of quantum physics we are already in more than one realm simultaneously. So why not take a short break to check in with another aspect of my Being? I call it a mental health break.

Many artists, great and small, thru out history have also worked this way. I am not exception-ally talented yet I *am* exceptionally aware of my connection to the creative pulse from which All (or you might say God) births. You can be too.

When the student is ready the teacher appears.

What just happened to me?

Years ago I took a recommended weekend workshop with Robert Moss, author of numerous books on Dreamwork. I was late finding the ve-nue where it was being held, and when I finally arrived the workshop had already started. I quietly entered the old, immaculately restored

1700's house and could hear distant drumming. I followed the drumbeat to a room at the far end of a long winding hall and as I discreetly took my place in a standing circle of about twenty people, I had the sinking feeling I was doing something 'bad'.

A very tall man with untamed silver hair was drumming a circular frame drum he held in one hand, a drum stick in the other, his eyes closed. Everyone had their eyes closed. My Catholic upbringing scolded me right there on the spot. What the heck was this and what did it have to do with dreams? I had already paid the fee for the workshop and driven a couple of hours, so I did not leave; yet. I reminded myself that I am open minded and very curious by nature. I shooed away my childish fear and tried to participate.

Most of the people there seemed to know each other. They had a familiarity with each other and with what we were doing. I was a stranger in a stranger land. Each participant was asked what their intention for the weekend was. Some of the answers were vague and sublime like: "*to gain better access to my higher self*", or, *"to honor the god and goddess that wants to live through me."*

Oh what was this about? My turn. I hid my

shyness and shared how I had always had vivid dreams my whole life. I looked at dreams as more of a curse than not. Sometimes I could not shake the memory or energy of the dream off. I wanted to understand what they meant. Some people raised eyebrows when I said I looked at dreams as a curse, (this is dream faux pas, don't do it) yet I was welcomed by Robert Moss. The weekend was a combination of dream sharing, and lying prone on yoga mats to drumming as we entered our dreams on a meditive journey of sorts. The large circle of people all faced towards the center of our circle, feet pointing to the middle, during the meditation/journeys, and I, as the rebel I can be (and in an unconscious move of not sure whether I really wanted to be there) faced the opposite way. I also parked myself two feet from the door in case I wanted to run out. We took a lot of breaks and ate a lot of food that weekend. These dreamers were big on eating. And laughing. I liked them!

During one of the fifteen minutes (or so) drumming journeys, I spontaneously had the feeling I was an 8' hawk. Or rather the body of the hawk was super imposed over and around mine. I became unglued. (I knew I should not have experimented with drugs as a teen; this must be a flashback…many years later?!) I 'saw' myself dancing as a hawk in a Native American way around a fire. I felt myself start to lift up and fly. Fly as a hawk. Soaring. Wind whistling thru my feathers and around my ears, all the while, lying prone on the yoga mat, my body immobile on the floor. I suppose if a fire had broken out next to me I would have gotten to my feet and run, but short of anything so dramatic, I was stuck. The hawk that was me, and yet also around me, spoke. It said, *"I am your guardian. I will be at your neck looking behind you always. I will make sure no harm comes to you."*

The drumming stopped. I slowly started to come back consciously to the room and as I did, quickly burst into tears. I excused myself from the group and left the room. Concerned, Robert followed a moment later, asking me what was the problem. I shared my experience and that I was scared. He re-assured me that hawk had come to him also many years prior, when he first came to this country from his native home of Australia, and was re-directed in his life path to be a dream teacher. It made zero sense to me what point he was trying to make. But his earnestness and lilting Australian voice, as well as his complete faith that this was a good thing, convinced me that I should stay. He also seemed very familiar to me; from a place long ago and far away. I went home that weekend and was not sure what exactly happened to me over the weekend, except that I was never going to be the same again.

My Dreamworld Becomes My Waking World

A couple of weeks later, when life had resumed all 'normalcy', my little bichon frise "Casper", took off and ran through the electric dog fence that surrounded our yard. He ran to freedom and also danger as we lived near a very busy road. I was panicked as I yelled his name. A hawk flying nearby came towards me. I tried to ignore it as I looked everywhere for Casper. At one point as I stood in my driveway, almost in tears, wondering what the best way would be to go in search of my dog, either on foot or in the car, the hawk flew directly overhead. It descended down to about fifteen feet over my head and flew slowly in a tight circle. I was unnerved, but tried to remain focused on my need to find Casper.

Intuitively I had the feeling that this hawk was connected to me and offering help. This was not a comfort as one might assume. It was somehow connected to that dream workshop, damn it! I quietly prayed that I was not losing my mind. "God get this hawk away from me. I do not want

13

this experience!" The hawk nonchalantly continued his slow circle above my head.

As I inched my way down the driveway, he maintained his circling directly above my head. In a moment of anxiety, I yelled, "Okay. If you want to help and if that is why you are here, find me my dog."

The hawk flew away.

Discouraged, I walked back towards my house, convinced my sanity was at stake. As I approached the kitchen door to get my car keys and as my hand grabbed the doorknob, I heard the hawk cry loudly. I turned my gaze back quickly and there across the street, and off to the right, was the hawk circling gracefully again. Directly under him was Casper, sniffing around the neighbors' yard. I gasped. Later, after Casper was safe back home, I did not feel grateful for the hawks help. Rather I felt as though life was taking a turn toward the crazy.

I had no one really at that time to talk about what was happening to me. The 'unusual' started becoming the 'usual' in my life. Over time and with a lot of second guessing myself, I did eventually learn to not only accept my new way of navigating in life; I learned to honor the gifts that came to me.

My dreams though became even more vivid and often times disturbing. I had dreams of poisonous snakes biting me, my body spontaneously igniting on fire (followed the next day by a spiraling swirl of smoke coming from my steering wheel as I did errands. My kids yelled from the back seat to take the car to the car shop. I couldn't though because I knew this was not a problem the car shop could fix. It was coming from a different dimension than the one the car shop operated out of), my being a rain cloud that later rained, three native women teaching me plant medicine nightly for a year (and they spent a lot of that time yelling at me to remember better), bears chasing me, more snake dreams and more bear dreams and on and on. For my own well being, I needed to understand my dream world.

I learned that much of what was happening could be likened to shamanic initiation through the dreamtime. My waking life as a mother, wife, bed and breakfast owner, volunteer at the grammar school seemed like a good and worthwhile life. Yet at night I had wild dreams. A different life was calling me. I could step into it the easy way or the hard way. It became apparent that there was no turning back; my life was no longer going to be the same. The 'unseen world' that was infiltrating my 'seen world' was not going to go away for the convenience of social norms.

Chaos

My husband did not find this charming. He was not interested in understanding what was happening to me, or even hearing about it. Our already strained marriage fell apart.

The dreams continued with dreams of Isis and Osiris (Egyptian gods previously unknown to me), Rumi (ancient Persian poet also unknown to me, embarrassingly so), a tall man with the head of a Bull, the departed who had messages for me as well as the departed family for people I knew, and more.

I started burning out numerous electrical appliances along with computers, fax machines etc. At one particularly challenging point, I would get a shock from any metal which included my car, grocery carts along with the cans on the shelves, for an entire summer. I found the only way to temporarily subside the electric shocks was if I took a salt bath. The water dissipated the charge for a few hours, though it would slowly build again. My 10 year old chronic

Lyme disease was also acting up and forcing me to lie down during the day and dream, even more than I was already dreaming!

My life was a chaotic mess, yet ~ I was basically happy.

Growth in Myself and Family

I did genealogy research on my departed mothers' line to find how much Native blood there was and it ended up being much more than any of her four siblings were ever aware of. I went back five hundred years of generational research in just a few months. Driving alone to Quebec City, eight hours north, I went to Universite' Laval which holds all the records of Canadian immigration, marriages, death certificates and more. It is a treasure trove of information, if your ancestors migrated south from Canada, as mine had done. The knowledge of this offered possible explanations for some of my experiences. Maybe this was why I had so many animal dreams, and Native American dreams. Maybe.

I shared my growing enthusiasm for dreams with anyone that would listen. I also found I was able to do healing work. I received 'formal training' from Robert Moss, but most of what I learned came from my dreams. When I am now asked how to work with animal guardians, plants etc, I share how I was taught in my dreams. This may or may not be the way others should do it though. There is no cookie cutter mold for healing modalities in my opinion. Similarities yes, but no hard fast ways for authentic healing work.

My dreams repeatedly told me explicitly to teach as many people as possible how to work with their dreams. I have written articles, done radio, and had my own public access TV show (The Mystic Dream Show) for five years devoted entirely to dreamwork. (for which I won the local Comcast award for best host, as well as the director Lee Moore and producer Daniel Weaver getting awards also for their work on the show) It is a topic I have never found boring and the results for many that I have worked with have been literally life changing. More than one remarkable transformation. How can this be? The power of our dreams is how this can be.

I am very aware of my night dreams and have been directed to better choices when I have paid attention to them and listened. For instance, when I had a dream of my teenage daughter coming out of the woods, scared but alive I woke knowing that she might be in danger at that time. I did not analyze the dream, nor did I brush it off. I spoke with her that morning about choices she was making and that I was very concerned. The dream showed me it was time for a heart to heart conversation with my daughter. The promising part of the dream was that she did find her way out of the woods, and in her waking life she also found her way.

Dreaming a Soul Mate

I had a dream of a significant Soul Mate, (my life has had a few) years before I met him. The following is the condensed version of a very long dream:

Russia

I am looking at an old street and know I am in Russia. Everyone has plain white cotton cur-tains in their windows. They do not aspire for the fancier material things I notice.

I am then lying sick and tired on a bed in an unfamiliar room. A man comes into my room and dances slowly and gracefully in front of me. I note that his knees, especially one of them, bother him somewhat. He is very large yet moves softly like a breeze. His eyes never leave mine. I am mesmerized by this. An older woman comes into the room and whispers into my ear something about him. I do not recall her words, but I am saying, "It cannot be. It makes no sense." She later gifts me an enormous Russian bear fur hat that she has made and tells me I can have it and be a respected leader in her community. EOD (end of dream)

I knew to pay close attention years later when the man I had started to date told me he was of Russian descent. I vaguely remembered I had a dream about a Russian Hat. For days, whenever I could grab a few minutes, I looked searching thru my pile of dream journals looking for the one that held that dream. I needed to know what the dream pointed to. I had finally given up, when one night I heard a small whisper in my mind say: "*Look up on your armoire and find your old dream journal.*"

I jumped out of my bed and there sitting atop my bedroom armoire was a misplaced dream journal....and of course the dream. I knew immediately after reading the first few paragraphs why it was better that I did not know the dream right off, because I had forgotten an important detail. I had written: *I am in the land of Russia, the land of my husband.* I was married at the time of the dream. Unhappily betrothed, yet still married. And after a very long protracted divorce, the last thing I would consider was remarriage. Yet my dream pointed to the likelihood of that, if I did not direct my life consciously.

The dream was amazingly accurate in details. His home was lovely but humble. There were the white curtains. (many windows had none at all) His knees bothered him. He is large yet graceful. I was sick and tired in all ways when we met. His mother generously supported me, especially with regard to her son. But the coup de grais came when I shared the dream with him (leaving out the marriage part), and he quickly replied "I know what kind of hat you had."

"Hmm? What do you mean?"

He reached deep into a dresser in his bedroom and pulled out something folded and furry.

"Here~smell this! ", he urged as he stuck the item under my nose. "This is what church smelled like to me in my Russian Orthodox Church that lasted for four hours on Sunday and I did not know a word they said."

(Geez, and I thought growing up a Catholic with a Latin Mass was bad. At least our service was only an hour long)

21

I recognized the smell, "It is frankincense, and is used in many cultures to get rid of the bad and call in the good, so to speak."

As if not hearing me, and in his own reverie, he went on, " It is from Russia and my father gave it to me many years ago. It is made of bear fur. Unfortunately it never fit my big head."

The room grew very silent. We were standing before a large mirror.

Facing each other, eyes locked, he slowly unfolded the hat and with a quick snap, popped the hat into its' familiar round shape. Old dust swirled in the shaft of light between us. He gently placed it on my head.

It was a perfect fit.

Of course.

I went weak for a moment.

When we would occasionally argue, I remembered my Russian Hat dream that reached thru time to tell me of what, or rather *who,* is truly important to me. It was not so easy to dismiss my relationship with him since I had a dream like this.

Did I dream the future? Was the dream a gift from a transpersonal being pointing a way? I see it as both possibilities.

What matters is that I wrote the dream down. When we write our dreams down we are honoring them if nothing else. We are also chronicling what our future may hold. I believe we all dream the future metaphorically (symbolic) or literally. It is an eye opening and fun exercise to go back and read old dream journals. It becomes very clear how connected our dreams are with our lives at the time, even if it is hard for us to see in our day to day machinations.

The end of that particular dream of mine had me standing next to a large expanse of marshland. A giraffe walks up and smiles at me. It was a random ending to the dream and completely out of context with the rest of the dream, and also played out later in my life.

Bear Dreams

A couple of years later The Russian and I went our separate ways in a sudden breakup. Two nights before our emotional blowup I have a dream pointing to this possibility that I share with him. He dismissed it yet I was very disturbed by it. The following night I have a dream of a black bear sleeping in my kitchen, curled in a ball on the floor. I ask him what he is doing. He tells me, "Susan, you are about to go through many changes and I am here to steady your heart and to help."

"No! I have had too much change and I am sick of it! I cannot take this much more!"

"Don't worry so much. I should not tell you this, but since you are falling apart I will let you know it will only last ten weeks, and then your life will be anchored in its new direction. You lost your focus again in life and have put all your energy into someone else's life. You need to stop this now!"

At the end of the dream I am lying in a shallow pool of warm water. A remarkably handsome man is leaning over me, washing me clean in a loving way with the water. He is smiling at me. I am amazed this man is attracted to me and we start to laugh.

I wake from the dream by the sound of my own laughter. Yet moments later I remember the first part of the dream and I am scared. I overlook the water, the handsome man and the laughter. I knew the Bear was the animal of healing for me. I was going to get a healing, like it or not. I fell apart for awhile after the break up.

Crying every day. I was in a new home, new state and knew no one but my previous beloved. I also lost my job in the breakup since I worked for him ~ all in one fell swoop.

Though feeling numb, I started to piece together a new life doing what I love: teaching dreamwork. I held onto the promise of ten weeks till it got better; even marking off ten weeks on my oversized kitchen calendar. Each week that went by seemed like very little progress though.

I was too worried and panicked over my finances to reach up and look at my evolving story from a higher vantage point. Too bad because if I had, I would have seen enormous growth and progress. I was squeaking by, but I *was* getting by. And I was doing what I love and not giving my life and time to someone else's' dream.

Giraffe Dream Man

Eventually I meet a man whom I had been avoiding and putting off. On our first date he tries to kiss me I tell him no. He is too handsome and wild and I know it. He kisses me anyways. My heart opens (again) and I felt swallowed in love. It is (and probably always will be) all or nothing with me. One day we are at a yard sale and there is a small shelf in the shape of a giraffe head for sale. (not an everyday item) I took it home and hung it on the cathedral ceiling in my living room. (kind of like an antlered deer head in a study) I recognize the giraffe from my dream years ago and how it is this man. He is 6'6" and could be likened to a giraffe, in size and coloring. I also recognize the marshy field that the dream giraffe was in as the present salt water marsh near the ocean that we go to. I never tell him any of this though.

A couple months after dating I also recognize he is the handsome man in my dream with the shallow pool of water. We have gone to rivers, streams, lakes, oceans, waterfalls, hot tubs; you name it, all for the healing and fun benefit of water. He has shampooed my hair in the bath, which I am now convinced is the best thing on Earth. I laugh a lot now too, like I did in my dream. I periodically want to break free from him, yet when I determine that is what I will do I have a dream immediately that tells me not to. I take this a day at a time. Broken hearts often function this way. Time will tell.

Chapter Two

REMEMBERING

"There is no safety in numbers, or in anything else."

James Thurber

'It does not matter much if we are winning or losing. It is all relevant to where we are in any particular story. Our lives are layered with story and to jump into any one point and declare a winning or losing situation is blindness. It is better to hold onto the knowledge that the only guarantee is change...better~ then worse, then worse~ then better...so on and so on.

One can only get this perspective if looking at it from a birds view. A flying bird and not a caged, songless bird. Rise up from the sadness and gloom and sing your heart song, no matter where you are on the story line. Stay fast and welcome the freshness of change that wants to blow into your life. Life wants to live. Life has an energy that is not static and any time we want to hold any part of it still, we cause a type of death. Do not surround yourself with death as you will when you cling onto anything near and dear to you. You bring into your life the sick smell of the dying. Dying wishes and dying dreams. Better to let the winds of change continually renew the vibrancy that wants to be in and around you. When you feel the clinging of comfort calling your bones, run the other way. Fast.'

My waking dream continued:

'It is trickery. Your true comfort will only come from the courage and trust you will need to be the adventurer that all Life wants from us. Humans are the only creature that holds onto things and circumstances. It is the absence of this activity that creates the inherent happiness that animals feel, and rocks, and plants, and the stars. They flow with Life.

Curiously, when we live as the rocks and plants and stars, we resonate with them, and somehow connect closer to them. We recognize them as the brethren they are to us and they recognize us clearer too. This can only be understood through experience. The experience is open to us all and is crying for us infinitely and infinitesimally all the 'time.'

Our primary business as a human being, from what I can see, is that we learn to remember. Remember all that we are. I am here to remember. I remember, then slide to darkness like the moon does as she cycles. I come back into remembering slowly as the moon does as she grows brighter, and I slide back into abysmal forgetfulness. Someday I may be like the Sun, ever shining, not forgetting.'

Note: Information given me in a waking dream.

Our lives and stories are multi layered, as are our dreams. The best approach to understanding this is non lineal. Putting one step in front of the other and proceeding in evenly spaced and paced steps, is not the way to approach dreams. A cycling, whirling motion is closer to creation and the flow of dreams. We dream forward and backward. We dream the immediate and we dream the potential. We dream all relevant possibilities.

THE POWER OF DREAMS

Chapter Three

WHO ARE THE POWERS?

"Poison is in everything,

and nothing is without poison.

It is the dosage that makes it either a poison

or a remedy. "

Paracelsus

Who are the Powers that speak to us in our dreams? It depends on who you ask. To many Native Americans it is the grandfathers and grandmothers that reach thru time to guide us.

To a Jungian analyst it may be an Archetype, as if there are many roles or personality traits that hang in the ethers of the Dreamworld waiting to live out their energetic lives thru a person that resonates closely with them. For example, one might have the Warrior archetype and be battling ones way through life. Or how about the Mother archetype in which the unbeknownst host is acting out all the many facets of mothering, both good and bad. We all have archetypes, (usually more than one at a time even) , playing along with us in our lives so it might be quite beneficial to self reflect and recognize them so we can make better choices and be more self directed.

Another source is our departed. Ask most anyone who has lost a beloved spouse, and you will hear stories of how the deceased have come through dreams for help or guidance or to reassure us of their love. One hospice group I worked with even published a book of compiled stories of their departed spouses coming through in their dreams. One benefit of group dreamwork is just this point: many had previously felt it odd that they had dreams of their deceased spouse. That is, until we talked about it in our hospice group and found almost everyone had very similar experiences. This is comforting to know.

Yet I am bothered by this. How have we come so far in our society in some ways and yet we think it strange when we have these types of dreams? When did we get so lost? Our ancestors knew what to do with dreams. Your great, great grandmother would probably not have blinked at the suggestion that her deceased husband came to her in her dreams one night.

We all breath. We all need food. We all dream.

We All Dream.

We dream from the moment we are. It might even be said we are dreaming while we are awake and dreaming while we are asleep. And many a culture has given more credibility to the night dreams than the waking ones. It has been understood from indigenous cultures, like the Kogi, that creation starts in the Dreamworld, then comes to us. The Dreamworld is the magical soup of creation that some of our sleep dreams come from. The good ones. Paying attention to our dreams brings us more of the quality dreams. Ones we can navigate with. Our waking reality shifts when we develop a working relationship with our dreams and the result is more synchronicities in our waking life. With time, we can actually feel as though our waking life is very similar to our sleep dreams, and we can navigate our life paying attention to the sign posts of synchronicities, as well as dreams. Reality takes on a more magical *and accurate* quality. We wake up actually. We leave the old life of the walking dead.

Another Power would be the Animals. I pay keen attention when an animal shows up in my dream. Their presence can be likened to an archetype, only of the animal kingdom. This is ancient and I guess more resonate with our genetics then the colder, more intellectual pursuit of a Jungian archetype.

For example, if I have repeated dreams of a snake, I know that for me, big transformation is brewing. The following is a dream I had years back that was an initiatory dream:

Rattlesnake

A short, surly old Native American man is standing very close to me which is irritating because I suspect he is up to something 'shady.' He tells me, "Relax, I am not being sneaky." *Moments later I find myself smacking my tongue against the roof of my mouth trying to discern the funky taste. The realization that it is rattlesnake I taste fills me with terror. I see the smirking man holding a rattlesnake to my upper arm, its jaws closed tight, puncturing my skin and filling me with its venom. As I glare back at him, he says,* "Stop your fear! You can handle this poison. Your ability to handle this is what keeps you able to handle other poisons in your life. You can now help others with the poisons in their lives too." *EOD*

I have had a disproportionate amount of poison and garbage in my personal life, and up to date (thank God) have been able to always bounce back to a more healthy way of living. It is not that I have vices or addictions myself, but I have been in some extreme situations thru out my life.

I am also able to go deep with clients and find the murky crap they had hoped to forget about and help bring it out to the light, where everything is less scary when this can be done. Healing can now take place. Rattlesnake venom must be helping me.

The Native man in my dream was right. I needed to recognize this in myself and step up to the plate. We all would help our World enormously if we recognized our power and strengths and lived up to them. This is not being egotistical, but instead responsible.

Exercise: Dismiss no dream, even a snippet of a dream. Have faith that help is coming to you via your dreams; and your ability to receive it will be in direct proportion to how well you listen. With a little time and effort you can be a strong dreamer!

Chapter Four

ALIEN DREAMS

"I hope you have not been leading a double life, pre-tending to be wicked and being really good all the time. That would be hypocrisy."

Oscar Wilde

There is a primary reason that I became in-volved in the study of dreamwork. It was born out of the need to understand a series of dreams I had when I was 15. The time period of my life when I had these dreams was overwhelmed with personal challenges. We had moved out of state, (away from my friends and boyfriend of a year, long time for a young teenager), our family downsized from a large home in an affluent town, to a small rented ranch which required my sharing a bedroom with my sister who was a year younger than me. Our relationship was very stormy and required much more physical space for us to get along than our new eight by ten bedroom afforded us. Our dressers, desks etc.

all gone. Our bikes sold. Our parents' marriage hanging on by a very thin, stretched thread. Disharmony all around.

I left every day and walked a couple of miles to the nearby colonial seaside town to hang out and just to get away from the oppression and chronic depression hanging heavy in our new home. I met new friends and found a very nice life was waiting to be born in this new town, but that would take months before I would know this. I read prolifically books that interested me: The Rubaiyat of Omar Khayyam, The Bhagavad-Gita, Lawrence Ferlinghetti, Hermann Hesse, and more. I would go to the library and see what 'called to me'. No one I knew, or had ever known, read these types of books. My father, a southern gentleman and descendant of many generations of Baptist Ministers found this very disturbing. (though not really relevant, my mother was an angry, disenchanted, non participatory Catholic) In an act of book brutality, one day while I was at school, my father threw away my beloved Rubaiyat of Omar Khayyam and the Bhagavad-Gita *(which I had stolen from the library. The only time I stole anything in my life. I needed these books. Most kids steal food or clothes. I stole what my Soul needed),* He was afraid I was reading devil books, and *"Who was Krishna for crying out loud*?"

I was horrified. This did not help my frame of mind. I meditated every day (self taught) by standing on my head leaning against the door of our tiny bedroom closet, my theory being; it was a physically healthy thing to do to make my blood pump backwards. I was precocious. I was loved, but misunderstood.

Years later I met one of my former high school teachers in my late forties and he immediately recognized me. I was shocked and quite frankly didn't believe him. Till he told me I was the girl that was always carrying a pile of books that no teacher required my reading. (I did not read the required reading either. Needless to say, I barely passed high school and if not for a 'special program' to assist in graduating seniors I would not have received my diploma since all I did was read my own books of interest and paint in the art room) He often stopped me in the hallway to see what books I was currently reading. He remembered some of the books all these years later! Remarkable man. He also said he always thought I reminded him of Edith Piaf. When I asked him who this was, he suggested I research her. Later that day I did and the quick synopsis is: she was a singer in France in the late forties who had one challenge after another, primarily in matters of the heart, and yet never lost her enthusiasm to keep trying.

She was small but mighty. One of her memorable songs being: *Non je ne Regrette Rien*, a song he suggested I hear. In a funny sort of way I found this flattering, though I do not like that my struggles were so obvious to some. So with this all as a backdrop to that period in my life, you can see why the following dream(s) were especially not welcome.

Teenage Alien Dreams

For three nights I have dreams of being contacted by 'aliens'. I wake feeling exhausted and somewhat violated. Even during my school hours I could not stop feeling as though the dream was still continuing in my waking life. They hung on my energy body like an unwanted old cloak. I shared this with no one, except one high school friend. His reply was he often had dreams in which he was Jesus. I found this unsettling and secretly thought he must have egotistical imbalances for having his Jesus dreams. (I think quite differently about his Jesus dreams now) I did not want to be having dreams that were crazy and lumped into Jesus dreams. We swore to each other we would never, ever, *ever* share our whacky dreams with anyone else.

The third night, as I lay down in my bed, I said a prayer. I begged God for mercy that these dreams would stop. I forget the details of the first two nights of dreams but the third and final one has always stayed with me.

I Am Marked

I am standing on my head, upside down in meditation in my bedroom, while my family and extended relatives are gathered in the living room of our tiny home. I hear a sudden burst of fearful cries from them. I run out to see what is going on and can see that an alien spaceship is landing on the roof. Though I am a child of 15, I gather my strength and pretend I am not also scared in an effort to calm the situation. I suggest we hold hands in a big circle, and as we do, a shaft of light the diameter of our circle surrounds and engulfs us. We are frozen motionless in this shaft of light except for the vibration that is being directed through our bodies, causing us to quiver and shake softly. This feels as though it lasts for some length of time and finally it stops. The light retracts back to the alien ship and it flies away. I am in shock as well as my family. We stand speechless and confused. In another effort to calm, I say aloud, "That it was okay, no harm was done. See? We are all fine." (though I did not truly believe this) As I wave my arms in a gesture as I say this, I am stunned to see that my palms are red with Egyptian looking hieroglyphs, as if tattooed on. My heart sinks as I realize I will always be marked and anyone looking close will be able to see this. I am the only one that has these marks. They appear almost burned onto my skin. Before I can think of a way to hide this, my family notices. My efforts to convince them this is no big deal fall short due to my markings. EOD.

For many years I put this dream and the vague memories of the previous two dreams in the back of my brain. The way back, tucked under one of those squishy looking cords.

Crop Circles

Then one night many years later, I sat in a friends small herb shop and bookstore combination on a cold January night, amongst a handful of people attending a book signing with author Niasha Ahsain, who had traveled hours from the north to discuss her new book and accompanying card deck about rocks. It was getting late and my mind was wandering as I waited for the humble event to wrap up. My kids were young and I had to get up bright and early, yet there was just a few of us there that evening and I felt obliged to stick it out. Suddenly I heard her say, "*So then I had these red Egyptian markings on my forearms.*"

At that moment my life came to a screeching halt, and squealing, went backwards very fast. I did not like it. At all.

"*What did you just say?*"

In addition to my overwhelming shock, it was obvious I was not listening. She nonchalantly repeated her story about how whenever she and a friend travel to see crop circles in England (at this point I am already asking myself why I was not listening to any of this before, seems like a good story. And who can afford to repeatedly fly to England to see crop circles? Does this mean she is a new age nut?) they always have what looks like red tattooed glyphs mysteriously appear on their palms and inner forearms. After they leave the crop circle the images slowly disappear after about ten minutes or so. She has seen other crop circle enthusiasts with these images on their palms and forearms while they stood in the crop circle.

In that moment my reality changed. Period.

I shared (for the first time since telling my high school friend) the dreams I had when I was a teen. I felt some weird kind of relief that it was only my palms that were red and not my forearms also. As if this might indicate that I was not as crazy as 'them.' The author was non plussed, and the other attendees were only mildly surprised, which also made no sense to me.

I asked her what the consensus was as to why this happened, and she explained that though no one was quite sure. It appeared as though some people were marked by an intelligence unfamiliar to us. Gulp. I don't want to be marked by anyone or anything, especially by Unfamiliar Intelligence! 'Beings' alien to me. I shared this with almost no one. If I was going to 'marked' (for what and by whom I had no idea) I was going to be in the closet about it. I tried shoving this new info under another squishy cord of my brain. But it kept poking back out. Secretly, I also hoped that someday I would be able to afford to travel to England and casually stroll into a crop circle and glance down at my palms (unnoticed by anyone else) and see if images developed. I had a strong feeling they would.

Life and Time continued on for me. A number of years later I get a call from my friend, playwright, and fellow dream teacher Gloria Amendola whom I had not been in contact with for about a year. As we often do, we asked each other if we had any recent interesting dreams. She tells me a dream she had the previous night about how teenage girls are being abducted in the late 1950's in Roswell, New Mexico and are being marked and tracked thru out their lives by alien intelligence.

My friend was born in the late 1950's in Roswell, New Mexico. Thank goodness this dream had nothing to do with me!? I was born in Massachusetts.

Really I knew the dream had everything to do with me and I told her my story about all this up to that point. She is dumbfounded and feels the dream may be more literal than metaphor, especially after hearing my story. I am running out of brain cords to tuck this away under.

Exeter Aliens

And the saga continues a couple of years later when I move my office to Exeter, New Hampshire and find out that (humorously) it is the Alien Capital of the world due to more sightings by more people in this small, relatively uneventful quaint New England town. (most sightings were from the 1960's) The town even celebrates this annually with a one day event chock full of authors and enthusiasts from around the globe. In the gorgeous Town Hall they have very serious discussions on the topic of UFO's etc mixed in with the Alien Dance (at night and well attended by costumed revelers) along with alien food vendors and a treasure hunt to find the missing alien hiding in one store. Though he is a plastic inflatable, it is a fun marketing strategy to get more people in the local shops that line the streets, who see opportunity to benefit financially from this curious 'holiday.'

But remember, I am the woman with my alien stories shoved into the recesses of my brain, even though they are starting to poke out and wiggle themselves loose.

At the end of the day of the festival, I stroll over casually from my office, *which is exactly across the street.* I have waited till everything is just about over and people are starting to pack up. I have convinced myself that this is nonsense and really does not apply to me, but hey~ I love books and maybe there is an interesting one over there. Maybe I can even find an 'expert' to share my dream saga with. *Maybe. If I feel compelled to share my story after my two second walk across the street.* Crossing that street could mean I would find out once and for all what the heck it all meant. I was not sure I wanted to know, hence why I waited till the end of the day.

I walk up the granite steps and into the old building with its' soaring ceilings built in the late 1800's. It was designed in anticipation that someone (and hopefully many), would have something so worthwhile to say that an expansive space was created to mirror their expansive thoughts.

I walk up to an elderly woman that looks like anyone you might see in a grocery store and not at a crop circle, and I mumble out my dream. She replies, nodding her head off to the side, "Over there is a man who would be able to help you."

Interdimentional

I cautiously walk over to a man that is sitting behind a long foldout table, not looking too friendly or perhaps he has had a very long day. I introduce myself and tell him the lady across the room recommended I speak with him. I quickly mumble my dream and saga to him. Kind of like a Catholic does in the confessional to the priest, spoken low, in a serious tone and quickly. Barely looking up at me, he responds that his name is Phil Imbrogno and he has a new book titled *Ultraterrestrial Contact* coming out in a couple of months that speaks directly to what I am talking about. To hold me over though, he has another book he wrote a few years back, as he points to a stack of books sitting piled on the table. I am thinking his apparent disinterest is probably due to listening to endless alien stories. I quickly tell him I have a personal moratorium on spending any more money on books right now. (that was true...pretty much) He replies, "Then I will give it to you."

   "Huh??"

   "Just take it. It is no big deal. Let me know what you think when you finish the new book."

   I pick up the book and thank him, and as I turn to leave I ask *the* question. The most important question to me, though you would never guess this by my casual demeanor in asking. *"What do you think this all means?"*

   Long silence. Then his reply, "I don't know. But many people I have spoken with have had very similar experiences. The new book even has some photos of the Egyptian looking hieroglyphs. It would appear that maybe you have been contacted interdimensionally by intelligence unfamiliar, or alien, to you."

"Interdimentionally? As in they come through different dimensions to communicate as opposed to flying in on physical ship from a far away planet?"

"Yep."

It was clear he was done talking to me so I thanked him again and left. I felt a little better if the communication was interdimensional. It felt like I would have more control of whether I wanted to participate or not.

While reading *Ultraterrestial Contact* I often felt uneasy. Uneasy when he writes that many people that have been contacted (or even abducted) have a high level of psychic awareness prior. I have always been quite psychic. They also often have problems with magnetic fields, or rather magnetics respond funky around them. As an adult I have blown out many computers, fax machines, etc. It happens only when I am highly stressed. I have seen computers and cash registers at stores freeze or lock up and get funny images on their screens if I am in a big rush and stressed. If I walk about 12 feet away from the machines, they start to work again. This has happened more times than I can count. I have learned to 'manage' it by either breathing deep and calming myself or, more often, I will also walk away for a few minutes. It is less expensive then replacing fried electronics.

In his book, Imbrogno also mentions many people had imaginary friends as small children. Reading this I remembered how I had an imaginary friend when I was very small (about 4 years old) that looked like a star and lived in a doorway that magically appeared on the baseboard trim in my bedroom at night. I called him Star Man. He was about 5" high. I did not think he was 'real' like the people in my life, but I liked him anyways because conversations with him before I fell asleep gave me something to do rather than just lie there waiting to go to sleep, I guess.

I remember too as a girl standing in front of a rack of postcards while visiting my grandparents in Tennessee with my family, a feeling that came sweeping over me. I was in an aching swoon to go back home. I was homesick.

But home was a Star and not Massachusetts.

(Interestingly enough, my mothers' name was Estelle which means Star) A number of times that year I would have the same feeling of longing, usually if I was on a very high hill. This confused me and I did not speak about it with anyone.

Frogs

Since I have now shared this story with a few people, I have been asked if I have ever seen a UFO. This past spring two dear friends came to visit me from New York on the Spring Equinox Day to celebrate the turning of time. The day was unusually warm and sunny with a clear blue sky overhead. We hiked through the woods nearby and could hear off in the distance a strange sound getting closer. It was a sound that was unfamiliar and none of us could place it. Following a worn path, we came to a medium sized pond and found it filled with frogs, singing their froggy songs. That was the sound we had heard in the woods! As we stopped and stood listening, it quickly became apparent that many frogs were swimming towards us. Thousands actually. Within minutes the water was teaming with frogs, all pointed towards us and watching us watch them. There was not three inches of water anywhere that was clear of frogs. It was a solid blanket of frogs! And off straight ahead in the distance, where a wide stream poured into this pond thousands more were swimming in. I welled with tears. What was happening? We stood there transfixed for close to an hour. They were singing but we could not understand. Later we drummed and meditated on this and learned the frogs are asking for help. Help for the Earth and them.

UFO Sighting

Later on this remarkable day, I took my friends up to Salisbury Beach in Massachusetts. It is a quiet beach at night especially in April, but has beautifully large waves. My friends wanted to go further north a couple of miles and see the infamous Hampton Beach in New Hampshire, known for a lot of people and activity, as well as being a gorgeous beach. There were more people than normal that night around 9:00 PM because the day had been so gloriously warm. A few hardy people were even walking barefoot on the sand.

As we three stood at the oceans' edge looking skyward at the stars I mentioned how I was always locating The Big Dipper now whenever I was out at night. The Great Bear constellation. They asked me to find it and as we are scanning the sky a huge white oblong flying object, the size of three football fields, flew by in an instant. I felt my knees buckle and held onto one of my friends. One friend saw the object along with me and the other was looking the other way in the sky. It all happened so fast there was no way I could have taken a picture. I was overwhelmed by its sheer size. Hampton Beach is known for having UFO's. It is near the military base in Portsmouth and also near Exeter.

What do I make of all this? The only thing I am sure is that this is an evolving story for me. I am not at the end of it. I wrote this chapter of the book last, after I thought I was already done writing because I had no intention of including it. I want to share the process of how to work with dreams and I fear this may open me up to ridicule and my primary purpose of the book will be lost. Plus I haven't told my kids yet!

But then I remembered when I worked with a hospice group in Connecticut and how everyone was quiet when the time came to share a dream. Finally an elderly gentleman shared a story of how his deceased wife appeared at the foot of his bed weeks after her death. He was very reticent about sharing this, but when he did, someone else spoke up about a similar incident. Within minutes we were sharing dreams of the departed along with unusual things that took place after the deaths of their spouses. This group had been meeting for over a year (against normal hospice time constraints) and had never shared like this before. They were too afraid of what others might think. We are very closed about so much in our world and in our western culture. But we need people to speak up, so that others do not have to feel isolated in their experiences.

So it is with this intent that I share my story. Maybe many others have similar experiences, *especially in their dreams.*

It is also worth noting that there is an increase of discussions about aliens and what they might actually be. One woman, Little Grandmother (Kiesha Crowther) Elder of the Sioux/Salish tribe states:

"I use the term Star Beings because in my experience a majority of them are loving, beautiful beings. They have been here since the beginning of time. They have always been coming and going here, and as our energy attunes to a higher frequency we will be able to see these light beings who are of a higher frequency.

Soon all of humanity will be aware of their presence".

Robert Moss states in his book **Dreamgate**s: *"We are not alone. Once again, we are relearning what was common sense to our paleo-ancestors, and to many generations after them. We must get beyond the sterile black- and-white controversy between skeptics and UFO believers who think that extraterrestrials are coming among us in physical spaceships to conduct genetic experiments and/or colonize the planet."* Robert Moss goes on to speak about the ancient Vedic accounts of visitors from hyperspace appearing to humans for different reasons including" *because they are being called in. The Bhagavata Purana contains a riveting scene of a ritual at the court of a king. As the priests vibrate mantras, gods and Gandharvas and celestial seers gather to join in the ceremonies."*

At this point, my understanding of my dream from when I was young is about my ability and desire to hold a space for individuals to receive a gift from their Divine nature, possibly a higher initiation, which is a result of authentic dreamwork. And *if* I am visibly 'marked', it is that I see God the Creator in everything. We swim in God. We are God. There is absolutely nothing separate from God. In the vastness of God there is plenty of room for everything under the sun, including 'aliens.'

And if all of Creation is happening simultaneously, that would include the idea that there was never a 'time' when interdimensional beings or aliens (suit yourself) were not. I have a request that peace and harmony extend out from our home Earth into the grand cosmos and all dimensions known and unknown, and be received back in kind.

Chapter Five

DREAMING WITH CHILDREN

He who teaches children learns more than they do.

German Proverb

While teaching an after school program for 4th and 5th grade students on how to work with their dreams, I had the honor of witnessing a profound healing. This is one of my all time favorite dream stories.

The class' first assignment was to create a dream journal by decorating the cover of a black, ring bound notebook with crayons, markers, feathers, glitter and such. Each child was then asked to share a dream they had during the previous week. A quiet, somewhat thoughtful boy said that for the first time, he had a dream where he died in the beginning of the dream and it did not end but continued.

"In the past", he told us, "I have had many

dreams where I die, then I wake up immediately." He shared this special dream that he titled:

Spirit:

I am walking across the street and am I hit by an oncoming blue truck. As I lay dead, a spirit comes over to me. She is beautiful with a flowing, light blue gown. I check to see if I am really dead. She says, "Yes, you are dead, but I can bring you back to life if you can show me anyone that cares if you live or die." *Confidently I bring her to my friends standing nearby. But they are acting silly and not really showing much sadness over my death. I then bring her to a person that says* "Yes, I care! He must live or I will die!" EOD

I ask him who the person was that wanted him to live so desperately. His eyes looked down and he said he did not want to share this. I reassured him that was perfectly fine and that we only share what we feel comfortable with.

I then told the group we would learn *dream theater* which is a fun way to also work and play with dreams. This is an ideal way for children to understand their dreams; thru theatre and the embodied movement of the dream. It is also effective for adults to work this way, especially when they can access their inner child. This boys dream would be perfect to act out, with his permission of course.

"First let's talk about totem animals quickly, since a couple of you keep bringing up the subject and most of you have not heard of this before.", I suggested.

I gave a quick history about how Native Americans work with totems, and each animal has its own unique gifts to offer. For example, Squirrel teaches us to prepare both physically and spiritually for an upcoming quiet time in our lives. I shared that some totems are with us from birth and some we acquire during life. I also spoke about how the idea of totems may not be agreeable with everyone and that's okay too. I offered to read about the Panda Bear from a popular Ted Andrews book; *Animal Wise, The Spirit Language and Signs of Nature,* brought in by one of the students. She had found it at a used book store and had read it frontwards and back. The boy that had the spirit dream was anxious for me to read this. His focus was on this book, not on his dream. He had been trying to learn his totem animal for awhile but was discouraged because he did not know how to look to find one. He was hoping with all his heart it was the Panda.

"That is a good place to start looking", I commented. *"The animal that you want to be your friend with all your heart, may very well be the totem. Lets read about Panda and see if any of this agrees with you. "*

I read to the small group of upturned attentive faces, *"The Panda is a quiet, yet strong animal."*

The boy nodded in agreement.

"They like to focus on one thing."

The boy nodded again.

"Their babies are so small that they cannot do anything for themselves. They need help from their Mother to even defecate."

I looked at the boy and asked if he was a small baby at birth. He replied, "Yes, I was a twin and my twin sister died during birth." At this point the girl next to him, and owner of the book, yells out "I know the next part, don't read it!" She blurts, "The Panda has two babies but only one can live because they are so small." The room grows very quiet.

I look back at the book and that is exactly what it says. It also says that, even in captivity, the Mother allows only one to live because they are so labor intensive to take care of.

I am amazed. *"How did you know this?"*

The girl replies matter- of -factly that she watches a lot of Nature shows and has seen Pandas on TV.

I look back at the boy and he is fidgeting and somewhat uncomfortable. I asked the obvious question, *"Does this agree with you?"*

He replies, "Yes."

We all sit dumbfounded.

Some kids also blurted out things like, "Creepy!"

The boy felt sure this was his totem now. The book goes on to say' *"...it will be most important not to take on more creative activities than you can* handle." I suggested that he might try one sport at a time etc. He said he tried illustrating a comic book last year and had to stop because as he developed the three main characters, he kept getting confused. He would now go back to that book and work out each character individually and finish his book. Incredible kid. I am thrilled, but none of this compares to what happened next during our dream theater.

It is his turn to share his Spirit dream and he quickly picks out people from our small group to play the different parts of his dream. He plays the role of the main character in our re enactment. He pretends to walk across a street while another boy acting as the blue truck, recklessly runs into him. The Dreamer falls dead. While lying in a heap on the floor, a small, sweet voiced girl floats over to him as the Spirit and says the now familiar ominous line, *"You may live if you can show me anyone who cares if you live or die."*

They both walk over to another girl, lying on the floor, who is holding blunt scissors pretending they are a knife. She yells, *"I will kill myself if you don't live."*

He then gets on the floor next to her and grabs the scissors. He holds them over *his* heart and proclaims, "I will be the one to die."

The 'sister' grabs the scissors back and says *she* will die. They struggle on the floor, both in a fetal position next to each other, for some time. The group watches stunned by the strength of emotion coming from their two classmates. It is

not clear how this dream may end, and it is looking like the re enactment has taken on a life of
its' own.

Finally he concedes and says, "Okay, I will
live then."

We breathe a collective sigh of relief and
though I am overwhelmed by witnessing what
just happened, the kids get up quickly and prepare their backpacks since it is almost time to go
home. Children process stuff much faster than
adults.

I ask the dreamer what he will do now that he
understands his dream. He tells me he is going
to be kinder to his newly adopted baby sister.
He is also not going to feel bad that he lived and
his twin sister died.

I can only imagine the therapy saved by this
powerful re- enactment of his dream and the
closure he got from it. I imagine he might have
gone on for years with a vague sense of guilt
and pain, amongst other emotions; unable to link
them to any one thing in particular; potentially a
real emotional threat for him as he grew older
and more skilled at stuffing painful memories, as
adults often do.

The next week when our class met, he
brought in a large three foot stuffed panda bear

that had a tiny stuffed panda baby velcroed to her side. He happily told us that his grandmother had bought them for him and he had carried them thru out his school day all that week.

Exercise: Find a child in your own life and listen to their dreams. Resist the urge to tell them the dreams meaning; children often develop a grasp on their dreams quicker than adults. Providing an attentive ear will work miracles and also teach thru example, the value of listening to ones inner knowing; via dreams. You will be gifting them with a new ability to navigate in their own life, a most vital skill.

THE POWER OF DREAMS

Chapter Six

EVERYDAY DREAMWORK

"My future starts when I wake up every morning; every day I find something creative to do with my life."

Miles Davis

I am in my local bank, sitting across from a quiet, serious woman, while I open another account. She is efficient and swift as she deftly keys in all my info to the bank computer. She knows I was laid off from my previous job (this is a small town) and in her professional, cursory way asks me what I am doing now. (I can't be too bad off if I am opening another account) I tell her I am doing dreamwork, and that I teach people how to understand their dreams. She stops typing and looks over at me, startled, "What?"

"*Yes, I teach dreamwork. Do you remember your dreams?*"

"I have one recurring nightmare that I have had for years."

"*That is a very good place to start. Would you like to share it and I will show you a quick process for understanding them?*"

"Okay. The dream varies a little, but basically I am always running late and unprepared for a dog show. I have these dreams every night for a couple of weeks, a few times a year. It is just awful."

"*Well you're going to ask yourself a few questions. Do you go to dog shows in your waking life?*

"Yes, I show dogs."

"*Are you usually prepared for these shows?*"

"No. I am very organized in other aspects of my life, but for some reason I am always running around at the last minute for the dog shows. As a matter of fact, the dreams should be starting up again because I have a really big show in a couple of weeks. The dreams start two weeks before a show."

I have to admit that sometimes this is a bit

too easy and this was certainly one of those times. But I suppose it may be hard for us to see ourselves and our lives as objectionably as other people can.

"This sounds like dreams of the future. You dream you are unprepared because you are unprepared and self fulfill your nightmare. Would you be willing to take time each day toward making sure you are organized for this upcoming dog show? Just a little time each day could go a long way, so that you're not pushing all the work to right before the show. I feel quite sure your nightmares will end if you can prepare better in your waking life."

"I can certainly do this. Thanks! And your all set with your new account."

I stopped inside the bank a few weeks later and saw the Canine Dreamer. I asked her how the dreams were going and she brightly responded, "Great! For the first time in years I did not have any nightmares before a show. I did as you suggested and put time in each day getting ready…and it worked!

If we currently had a culture that shared dreams, I feel sure that most anyone could have helped direct her towards this easy and obvious solution. One does not need a psychology degree to understand dreams. Again, this is not an intellectual pursuit.

We Are All Dreaming

We all dream every night whether we remember or not. Are you not curious what you are doing with close to a third of your life?

Your Soul takes a nightly journey. It may go visit a deceased loved one. It may go revisit a past life. It may go check on someone you are concerned about in your waking life. It may even go live a life much closer to your true self than the one you are currently leading in your waking state.

Indigenous people have known that the Dream World is the real world and all that happens is created there first. How can it be the Real World? An example from my own life is for years I often had horrible dreams of my husband at that time. I would wake distressed or angry and had a hard time shaking off the dream. My ex husband would ask how I could ever be mad at him because of a dream. (I did not know the power of my dreaming at that time). Years later, while in the process of a very nasty divorce, I saw that my dreams had been telling me the truth about him. He was not the person he presented to me. Needless to say, my dreaming unnerved him. I trust my dreams more than my waking judgment. I am too skilled at being in denial in my waking life. Our dreams do not lie.

Exeter Office

Another time, I am deciding how I am going to afford an office in a town I recently moved to. I end up finding a great space nearby in an artsy town in New Hampshire yet am hesitant in taking it due to the newness of my business. Will I be able to bring in enough business to sustain the rent? I have a dream in which I am told to rent the space. I see the number three floating in the opened office door three times. For me this image is lucky. Three is the number of beginnings and creation and multiplying it by three tripled its blessing. Nine is the number that keeps popping up everywhere in my life in New Hampshire as I embark on the new chapter of my life. Nine is completion. Due to this auspicious dream, I rent the office space and find it to be a very good decision.

The Dream World will always give us the real scoop. What if we do not like what the Dream World is saying? More often than not, we can change the course of our lives to either avoid an unpleasant situation or we can direct our lives more to our liking. Of course this is much more effective when we are living our lives in harmony with our greater purpose. If we choose to stay off track of where we should be, then the dreams will continue to point us to a different direction.

And if we are stubborn and refuse to act on the dream, (or not even remember) then we might end up with nightmares. Nightmares are usually a louder version of a previous message that we did not acknowledge.

Dreams of the Ex

A woman came to me whose husband of many years left her for another woman; a younger, newer model. She had not slept thru the night in over 5 years. Every night in her dreams she saw her ex and she resumed similar activities that they did while they had been married. She did not want this and did not find it comforting. She actually found it disturbing to the point she was unable to move on and create a new life for herself. She looked older than her years and was resigned to the idea that the rest of her life would be a lesson of endurance till she reached her grave. All joy sucked out of her pale being. She also told me upfront she was devoting exactly one hour of dreamwork to get rid of this five year problem. We talked about how her life was not over and I strongly suggested she start living it.

I led her on a meditation, thru gentle heartbeat drumming, to a time of when she was a teenager. I asked her to speak with her sassy seventeen year old self and ask her advice on what she should be doing so she can get on with her life. A healthy seventeen year old has no patience for morbid self loathing of life. Nor do they have a fondness for letting ones hair, clothes and hygiene go. Her younger self wanted her to revamp her look, get out of her rut, and go have fun! Our seventeen year old selves are living inside us by the way, as well as our five year old self and thirty two year old self along with all the in-between ages.

Spontaneous Soul Retrieval

If we have made a promise to ourselves at any point in our lives as we go along, and then choose to live in complete denial of this promise (and be aware some promises we make to ourselves are whispered in the depth of our Soul, unheard, but by a very good listener), we open ourselves to problems. Self created problems.

If it is an important enough promise, we can bet that our lives will steer us back to our original blueprint, so to speak, even if it takes chaos and destruction to get us there. We often make life harder than it has to be.

Anyways, she took heed of her seventeen year old self and called me a few days later. She was thrilled that for the first time in five years she was sleeping through the night! Her ex husband popped in at one point in one dream and she shooed him out. Just like that. She was empowered.

Fellow dream teacher and friend Karen Silverstein shared this dream from many years ago, and it is a good example of how we can problem solve with our dreams:

THE MAGICAL HORSE (1997)

I find myself walking through a wooded area and then see the edge of a dirt road and decide to turn onto this. I am walking only a few minutes and find an old Indian man who is leading a beautiful Chestnut Horse along the road. Catching up to him, he stops and we exchange smiles.

I am petting the horse and admiring it. I try small talk with this man but he doesn't seem to want to talk. That was ok, and I was ready to move on.

As I am about to leave, the old Indian hands me the reins of the horse and motions for me to go and to take the horse! I think he must be mistaken and say; "No, no"! But he keeps insisting with his gestures and then points to a house that is at the top of this uphill road. I am confused, but he continues to point to this old farm house moving his arms urgently that I go there with this horse. Finally I agree and he helps me climb onto the Chestnut Horse. I think to myself, this horse is so similar to one I had as a young girl of seventeen years. I pat the horses' main and thank the old Indian. He waves and continues back down the road.

The Chestnut Horse is prancing some; I tell her that I have named her 'Chestnut'. She seems happy and I ask where should we go? And with that we are off in a flash, running like the wind! Before I can say a thing we are in front of the old farm house on the top of the hill. I am ready to get down, when suddenly, the Chestnut Horse walks up the steps and goes right into the house!

The house is big and strange I think and say that to Chestnut as we walk around. The furniture is arranged in long narrow lines and mostly made from metal. I was wondering about this when a short chubby man appears and seems to be trying to sell this house to me. He tells me about all the features and that the horse would like it here too! Then he says; "Come to the second floor"! The Chestnut Horse and I follow him up the stairs. These rooms are even stranger! I see many metal tubes and tall glass tubes and wires all around connecting this and that. I want to tell the short man, that this is a very weird house; but he has gone!

The next thing I know is; I am running like the wind through the fields on the Chestnut Horse! EOD

My feelings were: puzzled, perplexed! What could it all mean? Reality check: I did have a Chestnut colored horse when I was a girl!

Later that day I was home alone trying to learn how to use the computer. Having problem after problem, I was ready to call it a day. I went to my studio for something and a book with a photo of the Chestnut Horse, poked out at me. I sat down suddenly and thought of the dream from the night before. I knew instantly that the horse was here to help me with the computer! The old house in the dream... the inside was the inner parts of a computer and the short sales man was trying to get me to buy it!

Well, I just laughed and said, *"Of course, my dear Chestnut horse who was named in waking reality 'Copper Penny', when I was a girl, taught me all kinds of things!"*

I grabbed the photo and went back to the computer and we began again to learn something new to me. This Chestnut Horse ~ Copper Penny, became my ally through many learning curves with the computer.

In this case a helper in Karens' waking reality came directly from her dreamworld. This is neither rare nor unique. History is full of stories such as this. (Read Robert Moss' book, *"The Secret History of Dreaming"* to get a bigger picture of how dreams have carved many a path in humanities march thru time)

As an interesting aside I have found, time and time again, that when we share a dream from the past, no matter how long ago, it has a certain relevance and resonance with what is happening currently in our life. The horse from years ago is very accessible to Karen now and I imagine there are new things, technology related, that Karen receives some help with.

Exercise: Treat yourself to a beautiful dream journal and write in it! Dedicate a few months, at the very least, to see its effectiveness in your life. Draw in your new journal also if you feel inspired to do so. Loosen up and let your creative side flourish. You are strengthening the connection to the left side of your brain.

THE POWER OF DREAMS

Chapter Seven

HEALING DREAMS

"With the gift of listening comes the

gift of healing".

Catherine de Hueck

The DreamWorld told my dad of his heart problem. His dream spoke to him with the power of images. Images are, arguably, more powerful than words.

My dad comes for a visit to my home, a short mile from his, and tells me he has had the 'funniest' dream. He dreamt that an elephant was sitting on his chest. (strong imagery) Later that morning his girlfriend called to tell him she had a dream of him and in it I had called to tell her that he had died. In a cheery voice he asks me what I think it all means. With a very serious tone I tell him I think the dream points to a possible heart attack. He flippantly dismisses this idea. I tell him I want him to see a doctor asap. He did not like going to doctors...ever. In a desperate attempt to do the impossible I tell him I am not going to communicate with him till he does. He was in the habit of calling me a few times a day back then.

A couple of (quiet) weeks later, he stops by my home and tells me he has been to the doctor and was told that everything looked good.

I suspected a lie and want the doctors' phone number to verify that he has gone for a checkup. Surprisingly, he gives me the doctors' number and I promptly called him. "Yes, I saw your father and everything seems to be just fine", the medical professional replies crisply.

"He is having problems with his heart"

"Again~ I checked him out and everything is perfectly fine."

"I am no doctor, but I do know about dreams and when a person has a dream of an elephant sitting on their chest there is a strong probability they have heart problems! Do more tests. Please!"

My father and his doctor begrudgingly agree to a more thorough exam. Two weeks later during the exam (and after my dad has been swing dancing the previous night at a local venue!) I get a call at 10:00 am from his doctor, "Come now to see your father. His heart is 99% blocked and we are sending him to Yale New Haven Hospital in one hour to do open heart surgery."

I am stunned, even if I know better. I rush right over to the hospital to see my father. The nurses will not let him turn his head to look at me, let alone sit up, for fear that it might trigger a massive heart attack.

My father lives through the quadruple by-pass and even resumes dancing many months later. There is a happy ending to this story because:

a) he remembered his dream that morning

b) he shared it

c) and I was paying attention!

Another healing dream with strong imagery is from my friend Grace and it illustrates clearly again how our body sends us images of the state of our physical health when we pay attention:

The morning before I got sick, I had a dream of an army of big black ants. I was vacuuming them up, but couldn't get them all, there were so many going in all directions. Strange thing about these ants is that they seemed "friendly" in a way. EOD

The next day I felt sick but went to work, and felt progressively sicker. Days later I went to the doctor and found out I had an infection. I thought it was asthma.

I realize now that I was sicker than I thought, and that the ants were the beginning of a bacterial invasion of sorts in my body (maybe that's why they seemed "friendly, they were familiar to me on some level). That dream showed me what was happening before I figured out that I was getting sicker, not better. Next time that happens I will be on the lookout and give myself a sick day to fight illness off, instead of pushing myself until it reached the "antibiotic stage" that caused me to miss more time from work and fun. I also remember earlier this year, I had a dream of big spiders, but they got to be less and less throughout the dream. Finally there was just one. I wonder if I was battling something at that time, and my body 'won'."

It is interesting to note that in both examples it is the animal kingdom that brings the health warning in the dreams; an elephant in one and ants in another. Though not all health warnings will come in the guise of our animal brethren, it may be especially important to pay attention to any dreams with animals in them, for this reason alone.

Exercise: Pay attention to dreams of your body. What was the condition if so?   Look also for dreams of a house, or car etc, that might also be the imagery that points to your body.

Chapter Eight

DREAM TUTORING

*"I never teach my pupils. I only attempt to provide
the conditions in which they can learn."*

Albert Einstein

Write it Down

We can all learn how to understand our dreams.
It takes just a little time and dedication to reap
the rewards. You start by writing your dreams
down. We have heard this before, and it is because it works! If we write down our dreams,
then take action in our lives in response to our
dreams, the 'powers' that speak to us in our
dreams give us better and stronger dreams.
They might be thinking, "Hey, if she will work
with this little dream, then let's give her a really
good one to work on. We have so much ground
to cover!"

I can assure you, that you will never run out of self exploration material with your dreams. You are infinitesimally large, wonderful and powerful and if you listen to your dreams they will teach you in what ways this is true!

Okay, so you have pen and paper poised at the ready next to your bed. (I have a friend who uses her Blackberry to journal her dreams) When you awake, even if it is in the middle of the night, write down what you remember. Do this before your feet leave the bed! For most people the dream wisps away as their feet touch the floor, because we are grounding ourselves to our waking state when we touch the floor. If you remember even only a small fragment, write it down. It still counts and will help you increase your dream recall next time. *You are developing a relationship with the* mystery *within you and this requires a new skill set.*

A major key to developing this new skill is showing, in a pragmatic way, that you will do something in the physical regarding something from the non physical. The easy place to start is to write down the dream. (It should be noted that in extreme cases of chronic no dream recall, and this *rarely* happens by the way, you could also just make it up to get the ball rolling. That's right, write a quick paragraph or two of what you wish would have been your dream in the night.

This can loosen things up enough to enable dream recall.)

It should be noted that when I first started doing this, I would dutifully write down every dream. From the first night on, I was writing down eight or more dreams. I was waking exhausted and knew I needed a new plan. I made an agreement with myself (My Self), that I would only 'work' with the most recent dream I had upon waking, even if I could remember previous ones from the night. I remained disciplined, knowing that if an earlier dream was important enough, it would come back to me another night. This technique has worked marvelously for me.

Loosening Consciousness

As an aside, I have never needed an alarm clock to wake up. Even when my children were young and occasionally sick, requiring me to get up a few times in the night to give them medicine or to check on them, I never used an alarm clock. I just need to look at the clock right before I lay down and quietly remind myself what time I need to wake up, and that's it. I fall as-

*leep, secure in knowing I will wake at the exact
minute I need to. I have no idea how this works,
especially since I am not looking at a clock while
I sleep. Or am I? Is an aspect of my being floating around and keeping watch over me? Appar-
ently so.*

Somehow I know this is tied to a healthy loosening of my consciousness. We do not want
an overly constrained and confined understanding of ourselves. You might try to loosen up
your consciousness in a similar way to help improve your dream recall and ability to understand life on more than one level.

Lucid Dreaming

There is a recognized technique for improv-
ing ones' ability to acquire lucid states of dreaming that involve asking yourself throughout the
day at random times, "Am I in a dream now?" I
offer that once you are actively working with
your dreams this will come naturally, as you will
clearly see events in your waking life rhyming
with your sleeping life. Consequently while you
are dreaming, you can have the experience of
knowing you are in a dream, while in the dream;
a coveted lucid dream. This can happen spon-

taneously and with some frequency.

Why should we aspire for this experience? Because when we can do this, we are increasing our level of awareness exponentially and the benefit is the ability to greater direct and create within our lives. Create, not control.

All the positive thinking and repeated affirmations in the world, pale in comparison, to the results we get in our own co-creation when we are able to lucid dream while asleep and active dream while awake.

Now that you have a dream or two in your dream journal you can start to harvest. That did not take long.

Dream Practice

Find a quiet spot with uninterrupted time of about ten minutes. Read your dream quietly to yourself, and as you do, bring your focus to the images that were in your dream. Closing your eyes helps, and slowing your pace also helps. You are letting yourself sink into the dream state. Your mind is drifting down as a flower might sink, slowly on the ocean. Your Being is like the ocean and over time you will come to this uncharted territory with familiarity and ease.

1) Ask yourself a few questions while in your dream reverie state: Does this dream have recognizable elements from your waking life? *(the extreme is, if we lived our life by rote, our dreams would more often than not, be a rehash of the day's events. I can think of no greater hell that doing the same thing 24/7, like in the movie Groundhog Day)*

2) Could this be a dream of the future? *(since we dream possible futures all the time, the answer can often be yes)*

3) What is the feeling in the dream? *(It may sound horrible to be falling off a cliff but if the feeling in the dream is one of joy as opposed to horror, it points the dream in a much different direction. The feelings associated with the dream are the biggest indicators of its meaning)*

Now you can piece together the dream. I love when a dream has a random image in it. The bizarre is actually easier to understand from my perspective. I know that somewhere deep inside me I made a connection to that thing or image along my way and my job is to go fishing in the depth of my being to find it. It is not hard to find. It was just in my dream.

Our dreams do not want to trick us or drag us around on a wild goose chase. They yearn to be understood. The image that is so random or bizarre in your dream is the best way for your Self to present the deepest meaning to you.

Dreams are our deepest level of truth.

This whole process can usually be done in under ten minutes or so. If it is a really Big Dream, the kind that you will remember years later, then a deeper process is called for. (See Chapter 15; Shamanic Dreaming) But let's stick with most everyday dreams right now.

With your intention you swam into your dream, looked around and hopefully now have clarity as to what it means. At this point we come to the final step in this process: dream honoring.

*Exercise: Keep your eye out for anything un-
usual today, and then ask yourself: If this were a
dream what would it mean to me? Pay special
attention to anything that resonates or rhymes
with a recent sleep dream.*

*Ask yourself: If this is a dream, can I change
parts that I do not like, or create what I do want?*

Chapter Nine

DREAM HONORING

"An ounce of action is worth a ton of theory."

Friedrich Engels

Spending time understanding your dreams is powerful and you can better navigate your life with this practice, but if this is where you leave off, you will be missing out on a key part of dreamwork: honoring the dream. Honoring a dream brings it's gift and energy into your waking reality. We can pull our dream world into our waking world, and when we effectively do this, we are creating the highest form of magic.

We can bring the Unseen world into the Seen.

It is then that synchronicities start to multiply and we can see that there is a higher hand(s) helping us direct the course of our life. Our waking life becomes more like a dream and our dreaming life becomes more awake. We are loosening up our overly constrained consciousness and letting flow 'what wants to' naturally.

How do we honor a dream? Is it not enough to write it down and understand it's meaning? Yes, this is good but taking it to a deeper level is better.

Let's say that I have a dream in which a Bear comes and offers me healing. I could honor this dream in many different ways including putting a picture of a Bear on my fridge, purchasing a small bear statue, reading a book about bears, or donating to a wildlife fund for bears etc. The goal is to leave reminders that allow a relationship to take hold between us and the dream, or the significant message from the dream.

The most practical, pragmatic gesture is the one that succeeds in this. Grand intentions (much like New Year Eves resolutions) are watered down in effectiveness. Do not honor a dream with intentions like: I will be more peaceful, or I will try to live more authentically, etc. Your Soul is yawning listening to this verbiage. Physical action is key. I cannot overstate this.

And, in almost no time at all, you will be living

a more creative and intuitive life, and feeling like maybe you can direct the course of your life better. We might even be able to live in better harmony with those that we share this planet with, including our dear Mother Earth. All this for the little time invested, it is free, and is gifted to you every night.

Lightning Dreamwork

Lets' go over this concisely in a method that Robert Moss created years ago and he calls his Lightning Dreamwork Method:

1) Title the dream

2) Reality check: do you recognize elements in your daily life?

3) Are you dreaming a possible future?

4) What is the feeling(s) in the dream?

5) How are you going to honor the dream?

I want to backtrack a bit and talk about titling the dream. This is an important step as it puts the dream in the context of a story.

Exercise: After honoring a dream, pay special attention for positive confirmation from the Universe. It is best to journal and track these experiences, especially in the beginning, to develop confidence in the process and validation that it works.

Chapter Ten

DREAM TITLING

"All things are passing. God never changeth."

St Teresa of Avila

When you title your dream do it quick and without angst.   You want a title that if you go looking
for this dream six months from now you could
immediately recognize it from the title alone.
The title also holds the energy, so to speak, of
the dream. Big arrows point to the meaning of
the dream from the title, (along with the feelings). Do not try to trick yourself into giving the
dream a different title than the one it should
have, with the hopes of redirecting the dreams
energy. (ex: I did not want to deal with a dream
about abandonment so I changed the title hoping it would make the dream not so) It doesn't

work and I speak from experience. Stick with the first title that pops in your head. Date your dream too. Interesting 'date synchronicities' are often at play that are best observed months or years after the dream, and you can only learn about later when leafing through your old dream journals. Ideally, we might even be so organized as to have the dream titles and dates at the end of each dream journal, an index, making it easy to find any particular dream. As time goes on, and you quickly realize how precognitive many of your dreams have been, you will find this extra effort in cataloging immensely helpful.

In addition to *making your dream a story* by titling it, you are putting yourself naturally in the 'witness position' of your dream/life. In many different meditation practices, we strive to put ourselves as witness to our life.

We let go of the daily march of life and let it roll along in front of our attention, while we watch; unattached to it *and the outcome*. The fruit of this effort is that while we are in this witness perspective we connect with our Divine nature: The unchanging element of our Being.

St Teresa of Avila puts this beautifully;

Let nothing disturb thee, nothing affright thee

All things are passing, God never changeth

Patient endurance, attaineth to all things

who God possesseth

In nothing is wanting, alone God sufficeth.

Looking at our dreams in this way develops the skill to look at our life as a story. It is an easy method for accomplishing the witness perspective and flowing effortlessly into this state of grace.

It is also a healthy way to look at our life. We are all living a story. Do you like yours? If not, what can you change?

Exercise: After collecting many dream titles start to look for a pattern. Is there one animal or situation that keeps reappearing? Make note of any continuity in your dreams over a few months period. It can point out the overall pattern operating in your life for that time period. A sort of birds eye view.

Chapter Eleven

DREAMS OF OUR DEPARTED

"While you are not able to serve men, how can you serve spirits of the dead? While you do not know life, how can you know about death?" Confucius

We dream with our deceased relatives and ancestors. They reach us smoothly and easily when we are out and about in the dreamworld. Most of these dreams are reassurance that they still exist on some level of being.

In a dream I had many years ago I am clearly shown this:

Bobchi

I am being chased by something flying thru the air in my living room. Though it appears to be a woman, in a flowing gown, it is hard to dis-

103

cern her face due to the speed of her flight. I am also flying in a circular pattern trying to get away. This chase seems as though it goes all thru the night. Exhausted, I finally yell, "Who are you and why are you chasing me?" She replies," I am your husband's great grandmother, and I have something important to tell you!" I cynically ask, "How do I know you are really the great grandmother of my husband?" (I am cynical often in my dreams and I feel that can be healthy. Why believe everything at face value? I may even be more cynical in my dreaming life than my waking)

In response to my question, she suddenly bursts into a ball of white light that fills the room and blinds me. Eyes shut tightly closed, I agree she is who she claims to be. I ask her what it is she wants to tell me. She replies, " You have been doing the genealogy on this side of the family and you are wrong about an important detail. You have two pictures hanging in the hallway that you are incorrect about who they are. In one photo is a woman kneeling with three small children around her. This is the grandmother of those children, your husbands' mother, aunt and uncle are the children.

In the photo next to that one is an older woman sitting in a chair with the same three children around her. The children are the same *age in each photo. The pictures were taken the same day though you did not know this. I am the woman in the second photo, the great grandmother, and yet for years you have always called me also the grandmother. How could these children possibly have two grandmothers from the same line?" I apologized for the misunderstanding. She also told me," By the way, tell your husband I love him and watch over him, though he has never met me." I agreed. EOD*

When I woke from this dream I went to the hall and stood in front of the wall of photos. There in front of me were the two photos from my dream. Shockingly, it was obvious that I had been wrong all those years and these were two distinct women. How could I have never noticed this before, nor anyone I had shown the photos to?

Even more shocking was this strong and determined woman reached thru the veil, (easy access in a dream) to set the record straight and most remarkable of all to let her great grandson know that she knew him, and loved him~ though they had never 'met.'

This begs the question: *Are only people we meet in life one's that can know us? Or can an-*

cestors and others also know and love us?

Here are two dreams my dear friend Daniel had, that helped him understand the state of his sisters' transition to the other side:

"My sister, Cindy, was in Lung and Brain cancer hell in our small hometown in Meadville, PA. On a trip from Connecticut , I was stunned to see her so sick in the hospital bed looking bloated, irritable, having lost most of her hair, so different than the vibrant bundle of energy, humor and love I once knew. We'd always had such a strong bond, and she asked me if I would help her write her obituary. It was important to her to leave her legacy, and I considered it an honor. One of the areas where we sparred in the past was her smoking; she held a black belt, consuming 2 plus packs a day. I was able to let go of that fight, and will never forget the day that, as sick as she was, when she asked me to wheel her from her bed up to the hospital smoking lounge. It was during that ride that she told me, "It won't be much time now." I knew then she was preparing me for her transition.

I left the hospital sad but prepared. The week before she died I had two dreams. In the first, I remember little of the visuals'; it is the voice that still radiates:"

As if coming over a loudspeaker, my sister muted the rest of the sounds in the dream and announced that her time was close. I have been a TV producer for 30 years, it was as if she had taken all the main dialogue out of the video and had added new narration, all the focus was on her words. EOD

"It was powerful and another sign to me she was close to dying. Then a few days later I had the following dream":

I am in the house with my mother and my other sister, and we are discussing Cindy and how concerned we are about her. I don't recognize the home, but it is cozy and we are all in a kitchen area. The next thing I know Cindy opens a screen door looking very much like she did in high school: beautiful, blonde, slender and her wonderfully compassionate self. She looks at all of us and says, *"See I told you I was fine."* EOD

Daniel adds, "A few days later she died. I didn't understand why I had both of those dreams, with such different messages. It was a few weeks after her death that I was discussing this with Susan, on the set of our TV show just a few moments before we'd go on the air live. Susan offered that perhaps the first dream was to prepare for her transition, and that the second one was to know that her transition would be a happy one where she would no longer be in pain and find the joy and energy she once knew. It

*had never occurred to me. But those two
dreams, and Susan's wonderful guidance have
given me such a peace about her transition ever
since."*

It is completely plausible that Daniels' sister
Cindy (or an aspect of herself, or perhaps an
angel) sent these two dreams prior to her passing, as a way for Daniel to understand what was
to come and that it would all be okay. It is important to remember that dreams can travel both
ways in time, backward and forward.

Exercise: Who has come to you in your dreams? Was there some image or indication that there was challenge in the communication, such as talking via phone, or thru a television? These are often indicators of communication from the other side. Many genealogists speak of dreams about relatives coming thru while they are researching their family's past. Maybe try some digging into your own genetic roots to see what dreams you might stir?

THE POWER OF DREAMS

Chapter Twelve

ANIMAL DREAMS

"If you have men that will exclude any of God's creatures from the shelter of compassion and pity, you will have men who will deal likewise with their fellow man."

St Francis of Assisi

When I hear a dream that has an animal in it, my ears perk up. I know this raises the quality of the dream, without exception. For me, as well as others, I have seen the greatest of gifts come from the animal kingdom. Each animal has their own gift or medicine, and as with other elements in a dream, they are personal, and that is the starting point that I take when trying to understand what the animal is conveying in the dream space.

That said, it cannot be denied that if I hear a dream with a Bear in it, I know it is pointing to healing. A hummingbird tells us to stay strong in heart and have fortitude. Snakes bring transformation and also can be an agent of healing. Hawk gifts us with vision, in all time frames of past, present and future, and to take a higher perspective. Eagle calls for solitary responsibility to lead and be complete in our authenticity. A whole book could be written on this. Ted Andrews covers much of this in his book *Animal Speak, The Spiritual and Magical Powers of Creatures Great and Small,* though he does not tie it to dreams per se. Yet it still holds. A wolf in your waking world is the same energy in your dreaming world.

Before we pull a Ted Andrews book off the shelf for a quick explanation of a particular animal, it is best to stop and take a few moments and discern what the animal means *to us.* It is surprising how similar the results are though and the more we practice this the better we get at it. We know deep within our being what gift each animal holds. Genetically we really are very similar and we are bringing into greater resonance our humanity when we can truly understand the animals in our life, both waking and sleeping.

Animals do not usually curl up and beg to be petted in our dreams. They often are attacking, predatory, even downright vicious. Why? Because they are animals! They have their own rules about how to behave. We do not reach even middle ground of understanding them, if we are disappointed they are not acting in 'appropriate' ways. Dismiss the method of contact in the dream initially, and focus on the particular animal first.

Years ago, I had a year of monthly court dates regarding problems with my oldest son. Amongst a mountain of troubles, the police had also impounded my car, as my son was driving it on his night of terror. (that is another book!) Each month I would ask the court diminutively for the release of my car. Each month the court delayed the release of the car with red tape problems; this form was not filled out, that form was lost, or that person needed to sign off etc. Each month I accepted their nonsense. Life was beating me down though my worries about my son exceeded my worries about my car. Then one night I had this dream:

Tiger at My Throat

I look in the mirror and at my throat is a two inch square that has rainbow colors filling it, with light shining thru, as if back lit from behind. I am intrigued and look closer. I open my mouth, and

to my shock and surprise, I roar like a tiger.
There is a tiger in my throat, living in the 'rain-
bow box'. EOD

The next day I am at court, sitting quietly, waiting for the judge to arrive and court to start. The benches in the courtroom are about half filled with people either waiting to go before the judge, or to see the outcome of their family going before the judge. I note a man sitting a few rows in front of me who hardly moves at all. He does not have the nervous, fidgety energy like most everyone else in this high stress situation. I am reminded of what my son told me about people that have 'been down' for awhile. He observed you could always spot them because they do not get fidgety at all, nor impatient. They have a different relationship with time.

As I am thinking about this, a man in a knee length fur coat strolls into the courtroom with no small flourish, and speaks loudly, as if to be heard by everyone in general and no one in particular. I recognize him as one of the lawyers that has been at court every time I have been there. He is also the one that has found one excuse after another why I cannot have my car back. I do not like him. I also do not like how he talks loudly about the weather and his vacation, particularly in his fur coat and with complete insensitivity to the people around him waiting in court. We could have all been at a cocktail party judging by his behavior and remarks.

I snapped. While still seated, I looked over at him standing in the aisle and I asked politely if I could have a word with him regarding my car. He looked at me, yet pretended he did not hear me. I felt a surge of anger rise through me.

I stood up and said louder, *"Excuse me!"*

Surprisingly, as I spoke I 'saw' the rainbow at my throat, and felt a tiger speak through my voice, *"I have come today to take my car home with me and that is exactly what I will do!"*

Everyone turned to see who said this, and the lawyer stood still, not sure how to respond. I felt one hundred percent better and knew without a doubt I would get my car that day. And I did.

I was told later that since my car was a conversion van with a TV, the police used to hang out in it during breaks and watch movies etc. They left it a mess, but I was glad to have it back regardless. My only wish is that I had the *Tiger in the Throat* dream earlier!

Exercise: Remember a time when an animal has shown up in a dream of yours. It is especially important if the same type of animal has been in more than one of your dreams. It points to the likelihood of it being a totem of for you. The animal is either giving you special talents and skills or reminding you that you already possess these skills. We need to take special care to honor our dreams with the animals, our extended family on Earth.

Chapter Thirteen

TRANSPERSONAL DREAMS

Angel of God, my Guardian dear, to whom God's love commits me here. Ever this night/day be at my side to light and guard, to rule and guide.

Anonymous

There are dreams that do not have as their source any aspect of our being. They are not a rumbling of the days minutia, nor are they connected to past lives, or possible futures. They are dreams of help available to any of us from an outside source. Call them angels or gods or friends, but we have access to guidance from an unseen world. How? And can we call them to us?

It is much more effective to listen to them calling to us, than us reaching towards them. It might even be the only way to connect with the transpersonal *is* thru their initiating contact. This happens in our Bigger Dreams. *The ones that are calling us to live our larger story.*

If we fail to understand our transpersonal dreams, we miss incredible opportunity. There appears to be a crisis at this time of good people eager to help, wanting to live out their life's purpose, but tragically unaware of just what their greater purpose is.

They are eager to align their life with The Contract of Their Soul, but they cannot find the contract! We may go to 'experts' that tell us what our Soul Contracts are. (Certainly someone else has the special ability to see that which we cannot, and is so vitally integral to our very point of living)! I am here for a reason. What is the reason? Are our Soul Contracts hidden? Are we suppose to suffer a Universe that is out to trick us?

Einstein put forth arguably the most important question any one of us can ask and that is*: "Is the Universe friendly?"*

Are we so small and insignificant that all things important are hidden from our understanding? Absolutely not! *They are shown to us in our dreams!* Your nightly dreams will give you customized clues to your larger story as well as the best way to align yourself with it.

Your larger story *may* ask you to change the world but most likely it will be to improve your own life. I have found that as soon as I feel I have accomplished and healed some aspect of myself, another challenge pops up. This extends out to other lives I have had and that continue to live simultaneously with the one that I now live. I believe it is the soft and subtle that wins the day, and in the end makes the most beneficial change for everyone.

Indigenous cultures know that what happens in our world is created in the Dreamworld and filters down to us. If we want change in our personal lives or to affect a change on a global level, *we need to be connected to our dreams first to be effective.*

Energy Work

There is a resonance with dreamwork and energy work. Energy healers are well aware of the field around our bodies and that most disease is in this field first before it manifests in our physical body. The best we can do for ourselves is to keep our energy field healthy, which in turn helps us physically. Likewise, we operate best when we can see what the dreamworld is sending us. We often have the ability to change the undesirable when we can 'catch it' before it takes hold in our waking life.

There are many ways to clean and clear our energy field, and I leave it to the reader to research this and find an agreeable method for him. I suggest that you may want to start looking for a method that your ancestors would have used as the first place to start though. If they worked with holy water, odds are that may be the most efficient method for you. White sage? Then smudge yourself etc. All cultures had their own traditions and techniques for clearing away the 'bad.'

What is not as effective is when people take on another cultures 'medicine ways' because it seems more attractive or new. This especially applies to Native American ways, and I speak as a Native American. There are many people drawn to Native American traditions, with the misunderstanding that it is naturally more spiritually based. I am not so sure of this and believe that if we dig deep enough into our genetic and cultural roots and the associated traditions we would find a much different story. God gave us variety, above all else, in life. Variety of flowers, trees, weather, people and so on. We also have variety in healing modalities, and one is certainly not better than another.

As we have our own field of energy so does the Earth. So too does our full Self. The ability to heal and empower one aspect of our being impacts like rippling, other aspects of our Soul.

The Land of Myth

The following is a transpersonal dream I had many years ago, and it really opened the door for my understanding of the immense stories that co-exist with our everyday world. I imagine that many grand myths are playing out over our world and periodically, however brief, intersect with our lives.

Isis and Osiris ~ I. O.

I am shown a small golden book. It is resting on black velvet which allows the book to almost glow. I see the letters I and O. I do not under-stand. A voice says "I. O." It says it again and again:

"I. O., I. O., I. O. "   EOD

I wake and realize that these are the letters

for the Egyptian Gods Isis and Osiris. The Egyptian story of Isis, and her husband Osiris, who dies at the hand of his brother is the mythology of death and resurrection. In a version of this story evil seeks to destroy a deity, bringing darkness, and thus develops an association with the lunar cycles, in which the moon appears to be destroyed by darkness each month, and is then brought back to life. Osiris had been killed by dismemberment into 13 parts, each part representing one of the 13 full moons each year.

In another version, Osiris is dismembered into 14 parts. His good wife Isis wants to bring wholeness to her husband and manages to put together 13 of the 14 parts, but is unable to find the 14th, his penis, which was eaten by a fish (as an interesting aside; for some Native American tribes a fish is representative of the male phallus) With Osiris' penis now gone, Isis will not be dissuaded from her mission to re-member her husband. She may have even been especially motivated to get back this key part of her husbands' body, the part that brings joy and can help in the creation of life. Unable to find his original penis, she conjures a phallus for him, and attempts to revive him.

In some versions, Isis sings a song around Osiris until he comes back to life. (this is key and more than one shamanic culture knows the power of song in relation to Soul work and the healing thereof) Beautiful Isis grows wings and hovers over Osiris. She breathes life into him to revive him and they conceive their child Horus (the hawk headed God, the god of sight). Being simultaneously alive and dead, Osiris becomes the God and King of the Afterlife. The feminine breathed new life into the masculine and re-membered all his parts.

This is a story of you and me. It is possible for us to create and birth ourselves and the method for this is in this story, if we look with clear sight; clairvoyance.

To ancient Egyptians, as a life/death/rebirth deity, Horus/Osiris becomes a reflection of the annual cycle of crop harvesting as well as re-flecting people's desires for a successful after-life, and so the legend becomes extremely im-portant. Religious rites associated with the le-gend eventually began to take on aspects of a mystery religion, with initiates able to partake in Horus/Osiris' resurrection, purging themselves of past ills, and entering a new life. During the summer Egyptians held a festival honoring Isis and Osiris.

This dream called me to seek greater bal-ance in my life. It pointed the necessary re- ba-lancing of my own male and female aspects.

Our male side (irrelevant of our sex) is the part that is solar, active, creative, decisive and so on. Our female aspect is lunar, mysterious, passive, intuitive. We need a balance of both to function to our full potential. I needed to develop my male aspect to take charge of my life again, after years of an abusive marriage had whittled away my self confidence. My dream was also clearly about my own death and the immediacy of the rebirth of a new phase of my life.

Yet this dream also gifted me another layer, *as the Bigger Dreams often do.* The **I** and the **O** of my golden dream book were also the letters of the name IO, an ancient story of which I was unaware of till I did some online research. The following is an edited version:

IO

The myth of IO is told by Ovid, in *Metamorphoses*. According to Ovid, one day the God Zeus noticed the maiden Io and lusted after her. Io rejects his whispered nighttime advances until the oracles cause her own father to drive her out into the fields of Lerna. Once there, Zeus covers her with clouds to hide her from the eyes of his jealous wife, Hera who has a suspicion that something is up, comes to investigate. In a vain attempt to hide his indiscretions, Zeus turns himself into a white cloud and transforms Io into a beautiful white heifer. Hera is not fooled. She demands the cow as a present.

Hera tethers poor Io to an olive-tree and places her in the charge of the many-eyed Argus to keep her separate from her husband Zeus. Zeus commands Hermes to kill Argus. Hera then forces the newly freed Io to wander the earth without rest, plagued by a gadfly to sting her into madness. Io eventually crosses the path between the Propontis and the Black Sea, and thus acquires the name Bosporus (meaning *ox passage*), where she meets Prometheus who has been chained on Mt. Caucasus by Zeus for teaching Man how to make fire and then tricking him into accepting the worse part of a sacrifice while the mortals kept the better part (meat); everyday a giant eagle feeds on Prometheus' liver.

Despite his agony, he comforts Io with the information that she will be restored to human form and become the ancestress of the greatest of all heroes, Heracles. Io escapes across the Ionian Sea to Egypt, where she is restored to human form by Zeus. There, she gives birth to Zeus's son Epaphus, and a daughter as well, Keroessa. She later marries Egyptian king Telegonus.

♫ ♫ ♫

What is the point of my dreaming mythology, especially when I had no prior knowledge or appreciation of such?

Some very important aspects of our Soul need mythology and poetry, even if we do not acknowledge this in modern western culture. There is a layer of truth living thru my life, as well as yours, that can best be explained by mythology or poetry. I believe mythology, along with poetry, is a birthright stamped on our Soul.

At the time I had that dream, my life felt as though I was absolutely tied to a tree and tortured to the near point of insanity by people closest to me. The Hera in my life was a very jealous individual, though not a mate of an admiring lover. I was sacrificed to the gods in my life (who called me to live my larger story) and I later traveled far to a safe place where I am able to live in relative peace. For now. My Prometheses was a man that was also tortured yet generously offered me hope and strength to keep up; my oldest son, a young man at that time, imprisoned for more than 6 years for a crime that he had no real part of. Stripped of all his freedom and most human dignity, he inspired me tirelessly to reach for a higher and gentler way of life. The Argus of my own life was slayed.

Io married an Egyptian later in her life and I shall possibly marry a man whose cast shadow is a replica of the perfect body of an ancient Egyptian; long hair, exceptionally tall, wide shouldered and small hipped. But that is a story for another day.

One way I have honored this dream is I have painted on my front porch, my favorite poem by William Butler Yeats. It runs the length of the beam holding the extended roof deck. The poem is titled *Innisfree* and I have held that poem in my heart for over a century. I kept it safe and dear printed on a worn out note of paper, stuck to the right side of my computer monitor as a reminder of the peace I would be able to have someday in my life. When I crossed my own Ionian Sea to the land of safety, (beloved New Hampshire) I honored the journey with this poem.

When friends now come to visit me from afar, I sit them on the porch swing and read the poem aloud to them. Most are surprised I am doing this and not quite sure what to make of it. I know somewhere deep inside me, that by my reading of this poem, I am honoring both our Souls. A few moments of poetry goes a long way. Poetry medicine. Especially in our ever rushing, always striving lives.

The Lake Isle Innisfree

William Butler Yeats

I will arise and go now, and go to Innisfree,
And a small cabin build there, of clay and wattles made:
Nine bean-rows will I have there, a hive for the
honey-bee, and live alone in the bee-loud glade.

And I shall have some peace there, for peace
comes dropping slow, dropping from the veils of
the mourning to where the cricket sings; there
midnight's all a glimmer, and noon a purple
glow, and evening full of the linnet's wings.

I will arise and go now, for always night and day
I hear lake water lapping with low sounds by the
shore;
While I stand on the roadway, or on the pavements grey, I hear it in the deep heart's core.

In another powerful transpersonal dream I enter the world of the infamous poet Rumi:

Rumi

I am sitting, across a small table, from an older 'Foreign' man. There is a bustle of people around us but my focus is on him. He slowly slides a sheet of paper across the table to me, his eyes never wavering from mine. I look down and start to read the written words. As I do, I fall headfirst into the paper, softly landing in a landscape of mountains. I climb a mountain, swim in a sea, and have many, many adventures. Enough of them for a life. I live an entire lifetime of adventure. Then, just as quickly as I fell in, I am pulled back out and resume sitting in my chair. The man across from me looks at me unfazed, as if only a moment has passed, and says, "Good job! I am a teacher of Rumi and you have just read Rumi the authentic ancient way!" EOD

I awoke asking myself who is Rumi? I type

the name into a search engine and am startled by what I read. Rumi, a 13th century Persian poet and Sufi mystic, is considered by many, to be the most widely read love poet of all time. I read further and see the name Shahram Shiva has written numerous books of Rumi translations. I type my dream quickly and send Mr. Shiva an email, ending with the question, "*What do you think?"*

I am surprised when he replies almost immediately, "I think you have had an initiation dream of Rumi. Many people have had them and it is a common theme thru the ages, amongst people that really become involved with his poetry. It often starts with a dream. Rumi reaches us thru dreams."

I am completely charged by all this. Shahram and I plan for me to host a workshop for him in the coming months. In addition to being an author, Shahram reads Rumi's poetry at wonderful venues around the country. This was how, I decided, I was going to honor my precious dream.

Weeks leading up to the workshop, I often found I was captive to my own poetry, which prior to this dream was nonexistent. Previously, I would not even read poetry. Now, I could be in the middle of the most mundane task like vacuuming, and be overcome by the need to get out of me a poem. If I did not immediately write it down, I lost my focus and was unable to do anything, even very simple things. I could not brush it off till later in the day at a more convenient time. I was being 'bitched' by poetry! I was not too happy about this. Plus the poems had a decided erotic tone that did not lend itself to my sharing them with anyone. I lived in fear that my children might stumble across one on my computer and I would have to pay for a months' worth of therapy for them.

The poems flowed like water out of me, and in minutes I was relieved of their pressing burden. Burden? Maybe that is too harsh. Can a love poem ever be a burden? It was more orgasmic, with a building/cresting/ and releasing. Once released from my depth of being, I would immediately go back to whatever I was doing, feeling refreshed.

Finally, the big night arrived. Shahram took the train up from New York City, along with his entourage. There were massive speakers, a fine sound system, and an extremely gifted musician that played a variety of world instruments organically while Shahram read. It was late afternoon when we arrived at the venue to set everything up. Beautiful Persian rugs were rolled out.

The time came for a sound test and short rehearsal. I laid across three folding chairs propped on my right elbow in the center of the room. I was the audience. An audience of one. As Shahram read, his voice resonating deep velvety red across the room, I closed my eyes and fell into a reverie. Rumi recited poetry to me that night.

Small tears of ecstasy rolled out the corners of my eyes making a salty line toward the floor.

I wrote the following poem later that week:

RUMI

I know why Rumi came to me in my dreams.

He fell madly in love with someone that was not his choice. He was consumed with love for Shams. No one understood and 800 years later we still do not understand.

Shams was not the upright citizen that Rumi was. Shams was a dervish vagabond.

I have spent my life trying to do the right thing. Always striving and reaching. When I was doing this, where were you? And what were you doing?

Shams came into Rumi's life and turned it upside down. Rumi became a love poet, along with being a mystic.

I am a mystic. I am now also a love poet. You have turned my life and all its striving right around.

I write you love poetry I am scared to share with you. I do not want to chase you away with the intensity of my feelings. I wonder if Shams knew the poetry that Rumi wrote?

It has been years since my Rumi dream. Often I will read a Rumi poem in the morning; a love poem to start another day of my life.

Exercise: Read some ancient history. The transpersonal Powers are not constrained by time. They are constrained by boredom though, so if you are leading a less than challenging and exciting life, go search history as a possible way to stir the waters and attract interest to yourself. Stretching ourselves, and reaching for the near impossible also sends a loud signal.

Chapter Fourteen

WARNING DREAMS

"Do not let anyone tell you what your dreams mean or your life for that matter." Robert Moss

I have a friend (I will call Anne) who dreams pro-lifically, or rather she *remembers them prolifical-ly*. She has been doing this so long that it is second nature to her and she easily navigates her life thru her dreams. Her life is anything but easy, thus her need to stay in touch with her dreamworld for either positive confirmation of her current track in life or possible warnings of future events. Anne even travels with her dream book tucked neatly in her purse, a 1" leather strap carefully wound around it so as to keep the pages from becoming amiss.

She likes to give me a call occasionally and keep me updated on her dreaming and waking life and the weaving of the two, knowing I really enjoy being updated.

Before one particular visit from Anne along with our friend Mary, I have a dream a month prior in which I see Mary paralyzed from the neck down. In the dream, Anne is phoning everyone saying that our friend Mary is paralyzed but will be okay~ by a stroke of luck. I write the dream down and include that there was chaos and confusion everywhere in the dream. When I wake I decide I will not call Mary or Anne to share the dream because it sounds and *feels* too ominous. Significantly, Mary ends up alright in the dream so I decide to not share the dream to not alarm anyone with fear.

Often there are many layers to a dream (at least the Big Ones) and this could have also been a dream about me. I was unsure, so I did nothing. It can be damaging to share 'bad' dreams with people. It can be the equivalent of cursing them. Equally damaging could be my sharing a dream about someone in which something 'bad' is going to happen, due to I might bring it inadvertently to fruition via the fact the dreamer unconsciously creating it so.

So how *do* we handle this situation if we do

have a dream that is concerning about someone we care about? Furthermore, our sharing might help them *avert* a negative situation. It is best to do this gingerly, diplomatically and with a great deal of respect. We use the words *"if this were my dream"* as a preface to any possible suggestion as how to proceed with a 'bad' dream.

I always add truthfully, *"I am not the expert on your dreams, nor am I always clear on a dreams meaning."*

Back to Anne and Mary; since Mary ended up safe in the dream, I used that information as validation that if this was a dream literally about Mary, she would be okay. I said nothing. I did say a silent prayer for Mary though.

Weeks later both Anne and Mary stop by for a visit and while sitting on my front porch on a sunny morning we start to share dreams. Impulsively, (I forgot I did not want to share that dream) I mention I had a dream with the both of them many weeks prior. I jump up and rush back into my house to get my dream journal and as I return flipping thru the pages looking for the dream, I stop with a sense of dread when I see the dreams title: *Mary's Paralyzation.*

My friends are watching my facial expression intrigued by my apparent unease. I am caught between a rock and a hard place. If I do not tell them the dream they will be frightened that I am withholding the dream, and if I tell them the dream they will be frightened. I am acutely reminded of why it is often best to say nothing.

But I *am* 'caught' so I share the dream. I emphasize correctly that the biggest point and comfort is that in the dream is Mary ends up all right, and that this dream might be a metaphor for Mary feeling stuck in her life, more than an actual physical paralyzation. Again I say the words 'if this were a dream about me...." We move quickly past this dream to discuss other dreams and I breathe a silent sigh of relief.

Two weeks later I get a call from Anne. She is panicked and tells me she and Mary are coming north to see me. Right away. They know what the dream *Mary's Paralyzation* means. Hours later they arrive. We settle on the same porch and they share this story:

Terror

Mary went out with some business acquaintances for dinner and drinks. As she sipped her cocktail (and gratefully this was her first drink that evening and she was clear and focused) she noticed her drink was a pinkish color. She had ordered a Marguerita which is normally a light greenish yellow. Her drink also had some frothiness on the top, but still she took a good long sip. She was about a third of the way thru the drink when she felt violently ill. She managed to get to the bathroom where she proceeded to heave up her dinner. Her head started spinning and she collapsed on the floor. She had the 'where with all' to call her friend Anne from her cell phone and cried out, *"Come get me! I feel like I am dying!"*

Anne, still in her PJ's, jumps in her car and drives to the restaurant/bar where Mary told her she was. Anne tried to keep Mary on the phone and talking as she drove. It was clear something very wrong was going on with her. Moments before Anne arrives at the restaurant Mary's phone goes dead. Panicked, Anne races into the restaurant searching for the bathroom. As she makes her way towards the back she sees her friend Mary weaving precariously on the dance floor, oblivious to the people around her. Equally disturbing is that no one (including her business companions) find her behavior alarming. They must have assumed she was a very drunk woman.

Anne puts her arm under Mary's shoulder and helps her fumble her way outside to the car. Mary is softly muttering she cannot feel her legs. At the car Anne has to lift Mary's legs into the vehicle and seat buckle her as she is unable to coordinate this herself. She feels paralyzed.

As they drive off, both notice a black car with its headlights off, following them. Anne pulls her car to the side of the road. (not the thing to do! It is like watching a scary movie when the protagonist does the absolute wrong thing that puts him in harms way. No! Don't go around the corner where the axe murderer is!) The lightless car pulls silently behind theirs and stops. Two men jump out and walk briskly towards their car. Common sense, and the natural impulse to survive, kicks in and Mary screams, "They are coming to hurt us! Drive away fast!" Anne does.

Anne drives Mary home and keeps vigilance over her the rest of the weekend. They determine that Mary had been slipped a 'date rape' pill after doing some online research. Mary's foggy memory of the events from the evening also point to this dangerous possibility, since another symptom is forgetfulness.

After a few days Mary is back to her normal self. She is aware she is very lucky and grateful that night had not turned tragic.

What use was my dream, especially if I did not share it? What benefit are warning dreams? Some things we can change and some things we cannot. Most of us do not want to know what we cannot change. Really we do not want to know. We may kid ourselves thinking we do, but the biggest reason I hear from people new to dreamwork as to why they do not want to learn how to understand their dreams is: "They dream the future sometimes and see 'bad' things."

My stock reply to this is: "*Brave up!*" Most of our futures are malleable from my view point, and that which isn't, I accept that there is a higher plan than I am not privy to knowing about.

I choose to look at the dream I had of Mary's paralization as confirmation that the Dreamworld had a message for me. Though my dream did not help divert the dangers of that night, it did tell me that I am deeply connected to these friends if I am dreaming their future. When I did share the dream with them, they may have found solace and validation that the story was big enough for a friend (me) to dream it before. It also points to a layer of reality most of us are unaware of, let alone familiar with.

I find comfort in knowing how little I know. I want to sense the undercurrent of a larger story bubbling and churning along in my life, but I do not want to control everything. I want to finesse what is given me. I want a source larger and more loving, guiding this mystery of creation. But that's me.

Anne said it best, "Mary was pretty much paralyzed from the neck down, and there was a lot of chaos and confusion. In the end she was okay but by the skin of her teeth. What if she had drank the whole drink? She probably would not have had her wits about her to call for help. Or what if we had let those two men approaching the car grab us?" (it was probably them that had given Mary the date rape pill in her drink) Mary ended up okay but it was truly a close call."

A few weeks later Anne calls to update me on all the news in her life. She told me that her retina was partially detached and the doctors were keeping 'an eye' on it. She was feeling better and the flashes of light that she could perceive out the corners of her eyes (and this is what prompted the call to the doctor in the first place) were greatly subsiding. Anne also mentions that she had a lot of car dreams the past few months. I offer it would be worth knowing what a car represents for her in her dreams, especially so because the image is repeating. I share that for me a car represents 'my life' in my dreams. This may have nothing to do with what a car means to her though.

"*Tell me the most recent car dream*", I suggest.

Car Dream

"I get into my car and have a hard time putting the key into the ignition. There is a thin coat of latex paint covering the dashboard. After a few moments of struggle I am able to break the seal of the paint and insert my key into the ignition. There are flashes of light around the windshield,that start to subside as I insert the key."

"*Well Anne, if that was my dream I would think that a car might represent my body.*"

"How so?"

"*If a car was a symbol for my body, the windshield would be my eyes. My eyes are covered by a thin film keeping me from moving easily in my body (car). Only after I break the film of paint (the retina was fixed) can I resume full bodily movement.*"

"That sounds like it could really be it!", Anne says sounding somewhat relieved.

"*It would be fun to go back to your previous car dreams and look at them now with the un-*

derstanding that the car may represent your body. See if that image holds true for your other car dreams and if it is applicable. If it does, you can add that image to your personal dream dictionary of what a car means to you."

Exercise: Warning dreams are not intended to scare us. They are designed to inspire us to take alternative action. Try doing a quick scan of your morning dream to look for any possibility of a warning or alert. Do this for yourself, and teach others how they can do it for themselves.

THE POWER OF DREAMS

Chapter Fifteen

SHAMANIC DREAMING

"To live is the rarest thing in the world. Most people exist, that is all."   Oscar Wilde

Most of our everyday dreams can be understood with about ten minutes of quiet reflection. But there are dreams that require a different skill to understand them at their deeper level. Recurring dreams, nightmares, dreams of animals, dreams that can be easily remembered months, even years later; these dreams are our big dreams and more often than not, they are multi layered as well.

We can feel as though we know a dreams meaning, yet when we have the ability to travel into the dream, a whole new understanding is unfolded. We can travel into our dreams thru the use of a drum and a steady heartbeat rhythm. This is a shamanic method and is effective like no other. You need not be a shaman per se, to work this way either. Working shamanically and being a shaman are two very different paths. True shamans are not created at weekend workshops either.

For years I avoided the word shamanic in referring to this method of dreamwork, thinking the word had a bad reputation. Too much like demonic. People are generally hesitant about anything unfamiliar, and dreamwork for many is already in the realm of la la land. I use it now though and hope to bring back the truth of what shamanism truly is. The old lies can die. Gratefully, there are a growing number of people around the globe connecting to their dreams and waking up to their life.

Steady heartbeat drumming gently puts us in a state of awareness outside our normal parameters. It widens our awareness. We can reach easily into imaginative realms that would otherwise be near impossible for most to reach. This is not pretend fantasy but *active imagining* and there is a difference. We also can reach transpersonal sources easily this way. You could call them angels, or gods and goddesses, or perhaps animal totems. You can reach the ancestors; you can reach either way thru time, teachers in other dimensions and so much more. It is the primary way I receive any information regarding healing work. It is the traveling method for shamans since the beginning of time.

Yet we can also travel into our dreams this way. We just start at the beginning of the dream and let it unfold as it did in the night. Only now there may be a turn while in the shamanic journey, in which the dream takes on a new story line. You can talk to anything in the dream thru shamanic methods, inanimate and animate. You go into the dream to gather information, not to relax. I cannot tell you how many times I was quite sure of my dreams meaning only to find a much richer explanation when I journeyed into it. An amazing amount of knowledge can be gleaned this way. The best way to understand this is to just do it. A trained practitioner can get you started and once you have your 'wings' you can easily do this solo. We are also able to travel in each others' dreams this way, with their permission of course.

I have worked with hundreds and am always amazed that everyone can do this. You just need an open mind.

When I work with a group this way I have found there is also a phenomenon in which a theme emerges in relation to everyones dreams and journeys. I have no idea what the theme will be in with any group, it just organically happens and reminds us all of how connected and interwoven we are. It is dream magic.

THE POWER OF DREAMS

Chapter Sixteen

BENEFITS OF DREAMWORK

"Our beloved dreams are dogma free."

Susan Morgan

The benefits of my lifelong fascination for dreams and the dream world are many. One of the most remarkable is that I now look at people and life with new eyes. I can look at the *Soul* of what is taking place. Often I see the larger underlying story unfolding in the lives of those around me. My waking life is also my dreaming life and whenever I want to look at a situation from a higher perspective, I 'work' it like a dream.

Let me explain: anything out of the ordinary that happens, I stop and give it a title. Check for resonance with other events happening simultaneously with me, and use it as a type of confirmation from the Unseen. In this way, we can 'read' our waking life. It is also how we develop a relationship with our unseen guardians, and increases our intuition by leaps and bounds. In short: We start to wake up.

This does not mean I am a guru or do not have my share of heartache and drama. Quite the contrary even. I seem to have more than my share of drama on most any given day, but usually I can observe the parade of life with an appreciation for its' grandness and all of us players in it.

The ability to look at a Soul in process does not necessarily create the need for me to be an ascetic praying in a monastery. The richness of our Souls expression is varied and it is best to drop rigid morality if I want to witness it at play. I maintain my own morality but observe and even appreciate another's' life with a more generous acceptance when I can see the work of Soul expressing itself.

I have a friend who on first observation appears to be a classic loser. He was a successful stock broker who lost his job, home and more with the recent economic downturn. He now lives with his mother, and drinks heavily too many days of his life. But this man can tell a story like no other. His world comes alive when he is drunk and he is very convincing when he is telling you he will fly you to Bermuda on his private jet, or that he is an Irish Catholic from the south of Boston and cannot turn down a fight.

Most people find him utterly belligerent, but I find something about his Soul utterly fascinating. If only he could channel his storytelling skills without imbibing in the Belvedere.

I see life very much as a story and we the creators. Certainly co creators at the very least. In my friends' often hysterically funny and sometimes poignant stories, I see a man with a rich Soul indeed. The tragedy is his alcoholism and if I can find a way to stop tragedy in life I will let you know immediately.

It is also worth noting that this man has a few friends who will drive the distance to his (and his mothers) home to pick him up and bring him back to their respective jobs to spend the day with him. Kinda like a 'take along pal'. Why? Because he is supremely funny and entertaining. Because life has enough sadness and he helps us forget our troubles. How many people do we know would pick us up to spend the day with us, feed us and be ever so grateful for our company?

He may be likened to a modern bard, perhaps a troubadour. A troubadour with issues. *When I suspend judgment*, I find an extremely lively, active Soul at work in his stories.

Another man I met recently, an ethnic Alba-

nian, burned badly when he fought back the Ko-
sovonians during the war in Bosnia/ Yugoslavia
in the mid 1980's. They were beating his mother
and he fought back at the ripe age of *six years
old*. They returned his bravery by pouring boil-
ing oil on his head. Who are these monsters that
I share the name of humanity with? One look at
this man, now twenty one, shows a healthy connection with his Soul. His brown eyes bright
with light. We are drawn, like a moth to light, to
people like this who are very enSouled. The truly enSouled are not necessarily the righteous.
Our leaders can be enSouled, but too often and
to the detriment of our world, they are not. We
are already well aware of this.

Dreams enSouling us with all aspects of our
being. As I enSoul myself more, I see with
greater ease the Soul in others. I see the Soul
of their stories and situations also. The price I
pay is that I am also witness to much loss of
Soul; soul loss. Soul loss has a major role in the
wars and confusion circulating in our world.
Gratefully, one way to recover aspects of our
self that may have left (due to trauma and/or living our life in complete disharmony of what it
should be) is thru spontaneous dreams. A
dream (especially recurring dreams) can point
out where we left a 'chunk' of our being: old
jobs, old relationships etc. If you have had

dreams of this nature, you might ask yourself what part of you is still left in the past, then re-solve to bring it to the now. When we leave aspects of our self in the past, it diminishes our energy for the now. This is a major component of enSouling ourselves in healthy ways.

We are in this dance of life. Life brings us colorful and enriching beings, along with their wonderment, their spontaneity and we in turn, are also enriched. I have a more generous acceptance of people after many years of dreamwork.

Exercise: Try to see your Soul at work. It is easiest found in the doing of the things that bring you consistent joy. In listening to the challenges of others lives, as well as the challenge of our World, try to look at it as a journey of a Soul; and the accomplishments and challenges that are required for the growth and entertainment of the Soul.

Chapter Seventeen

SOUL CONTRACTS

"I am best when I am myself."

Susan Morgan

You can know why you are here. If you do not already know, it is because you do not know where yet to look. The most accurate place is also the easiest, and that is in your dreams.

Years ago I had this dream, among many, of my Soul's purpose:

Acorn

I am walking along a small winding path in the deep woods. Travelling with me is a small group of people as well as my mentor and teacher. I am holding in both arms an acorn top

157

the size of a large platter. It is chock full of acorns. As I walk along, I take an acorn from my acorn platter and hand one to each person I come across. EOD

It may seem surprising that such a short dream could clothe the purpose of my life. It is not the only dream I have had with regard to why I am here, but it is one of my favorites. The acorns represent the seeds of dreamwork that I share with as many people as I can. The acorn seed grows into the mighty Oak, the strongest of trees. The seeds, or acorns of dream knowledge allowed to grow with an understanding of our dreams that can help us grow strong as the Oak.

I honor this dream with a large carved wooden acorn that I bring with me to all my dream groups, as my reminder of what I am best suited to do.

Here is a powerful dream that poet and Native American Joy Harjo had:

You Can Change The Story, My Spirit Said To Me As I Sat Near the Sea

I am in a village up North; it feels like the lands named "Alaska" now. These places had their own names long before English, Russian or any other imposed politically trade language. It is in the times when people dreamed and thought together as one being. That doesn't mean there weren't individuals. In those times people were more individual in personhood than they are now in their common assertion of individuality: one person kept residence on the moon even while living in the village. Another was a man who dressed up and lived as a woman and was known as the best seamstress.

I have traveled to this village with a close friend who is also a relative. We are related to nearly everyone by marriage, clan or blood. The first night after our arrival a woman is brutally killed in the village. Murder is not commonplace. The evil of it puts the whole village at risk. It has to be dealt with immediately so that the turbulence will not leave the people open to more evil. Because my friend and I are the most obvious influence, it is decided that we are to be killed, to satisfy the murder, to ensure the village will continue in a harmonious manner. No one tells us we were going to be killed. We know it; my bones know it. It is unfortunate, but it is how things work.

The next morning my friend and I have walked down from the village to help gather, when we hear the killing committee comes for us. I can hear them behind us, with their implements and stones, their psychic roar of purpose. I know they are going to kill us. I know this is the end. I feel sorry for the body that has been my clothes on this journey. It has served me well. My body was a suitable house of protection and enjoyment. I hear and still hear the crunch of bones as the village mob, which was sent to do the job, slams us violently. It's not personal, at least for most of them. A few gain pleasure. I feel my body's confused and terrible protest, then my spirit leaps out above the scene and I watch briefly before circling toward the sea.

I linger out near the sea and my soul's helper who has been with me through the stories of my being says, "You can go back and change the story."

My first thought was, why would I want to do that? I am free of the needs of earth existence. I can move like wind and water. But then, because I am human, not bird or whale; I feel compelled.

w "What do you mean, change the story?"

Then I am back in the clothes of my body outside the village. I am back in the time between the killing in the village and my certain death in retribution.

"Now what am I supposed to do?" *I ask my Spirit. I can see no other way to proceed through the story.*

My Spirit responds, "You know what to do. Look, and you will see the story."

And then I am alone with the sea and the sky. I give my thinking to time and let them go play. It is then I see. I see a man in the village stalk a woman. She is not interested in him but he won't let go. He stalks her as he stalks a walrus. He is the village's best hunter of walrus. He stalks her to her home, and when no one else is there, he trusses her as if she is a walrus, kills her and drags her body out of her house to the sea. I can see the trail of blood behind them. I can see his footprints in blood as he returns to the village alone.

I am in the village with my friend. The people are gathering and talking about the killing. I can feel their nudges towards my friend and me. I stand up with a drum in my hand. I say:

"I have a story I want to tell you."

And then I begin drumming and dancing to accompany the story. It is pleasing and the people want to hear more. They want to hear what kind of story I am bringing from my village. I sing, dance and tell the story of a walrus hunter. He is the best walrus hunter of a village. I sing about his relationship to the walrus, and how he has fed his people. And how skilled he is as he walks out onto the ice to call out the walrus. And then I tell the story of the killing of a walrus who is like a woman. I talk about the qualities of the woman, whom the man sees as a walrus. By now, the story has its own spirit that wants to live. It dances and sings and breathes. It surprises me with what it knows.

With the last step, the last hit of the drum, the killer stands up, as if to flee the gathering. The people turn together as one and see him. They see that he has killed the woman and it is his life that is taken to satisfy the murder. EOD

When I return from sleep, I can still hear the singing, and I get up from my bed and dance and sing the story. It is still on my tongue, my body as if it has lived there all along, though I am in a city with many streams of peoples from far and wide across the earth. We make a jumble of stories. We do not dream together.

Joy adds as a follow up to the dream:

Here's a brief note about its' relationship to what was going on in my life at that time, and how it might relate.

At the time of the dreaming, I was embattled in a struggle against the university in which I was teaching. The, then director of the program and I became very good friends as we attempted to right a difficult situation, to save a program. A colleague we had to work closely with was on a sex site with students. They were involved in soliciting sex together. The university, instead of disciplining the colleague or firing her, supported her, and turned against those of us who asked that the situation be properly addressed. We were told that if we spoke up, we'd lose our jobs. They would destroy our program. I am convinced that the person who was with me in the dream was this friend. I told her the dream and we pondered how to change the story. What kind of storytelling would turn the outcome? I never quite figured it out. I quit my dream job. She continues to teach, but resigned from the directorship of a wonderful program she helped build. She, along with another faculty member now have a lawsuit pending against the university. I was awarded unemployment. The university, in further harassment, is attempting to appeal it. I was recently cross examined by the judge

and attorneys. That night my van was vanda-
lized and I was awakened by a warning doorbell
ring to frighten me to back off. I alarmed my car
and my house for protection.

In this challenging type of situation, we can go
back into the dream, shamanically, and see if we
can alter the story. We nudge it in a new direction with our *active imagination*, and see if a
more positive outcome can be made. We can
also have a discussion with elements in the
dream to get their advice on the best way to
proceed.

Having the dream is part one of a three part
process here:

First: we have the dream explaining meta-
phorically the current situation,

Second: we can go back into the dream to
'dream it forward' in a healthier direction if poss-
ible, and

Third: we take action in our waking life with
the information we have received.

The biggest clue that this situation is not rigid
and fixed is in the title: You Can Change the
Story.

Chapter Eighteen

INTUITION

Unseen into the Seen

Another benefit of dreamwork is that our intuition increases. The very nature of working with our dreams brings us to the unseen world which is the exact place we need to go to if we want to connect more deeply with our intuitive side.

This is a naturally unfolding consequence of dreamwork, and is best accomplished and effective without the extra striving that is required when we try to increase intuition and yet do not know how to connect with our dreams. I cannot understand how anyone can make the claim of being a spiritual person, let alone teacher, if they are not also working with their dreams. The *accurate* and juicy stuff is in our dreams! We are free of our egoic machinations in our dreams, hence making them more true than the 'truth' we delude ourselves with in our unconscious waking life. When you are connected to your dreams, your unconscious waking life becomes conscious, and thus you can be termed a 'conscious dreamer.'

This Dream called Life then becomes recognized in both our sleeping and waking life.

*Exercise: The more skilled you get at remem-
bering and going back into your dreams, the
more your intuition will increase. Practice the
'going within' daily, till it becomes second nature
to check in with your deeper self, then come
back out quickly and resume your waking life.*

THE POWER OF DREAMS

Chapter Nineteen

SACRE COEUR

We are all wanderers on this Earth. Our hearts are filled with wonder and our Soul deep with dreams.
Gypsy Proverb

Sacre Coeur/ Sacred Courage/ Sacred Heart. If we are aware (and *not* just an intellectual understanding) that the life we lead is a continuation of the dream from our sleep, we see life having more possibilities. We have a hand in its creation. Also, if it is a dream, then a lot of what we previously thought to be so vitally important becomes less glittery and attractive. Much of our attention previously spent on the unimportant business, busy-ness, of life wisps' away, which leaves us with the sacredness of life.

With our awareness focused on the sacredness comes the ability to see clearly the transient nature of life. Our awareness of the transience brings us back to the sacredness, the two ever looping with each other.

If I understand the ever changing, always moving quality of my life, and if I connect more with the sacredness around me, then I am inspired to live my life more courageously. Not bravery for bravery's sake, but rather from the viewpoint that if I am creating much of my life, I will create something I want. My dreams have told me where my higher purpose lies and so I can direct my life in resonance with my purpose. My heart can lead me to bravely pursue the highest use of my precious life.

And when I am generous of Spirit with myself, it automatically pours forth into the lives of those around me. I am more generous and tolerant with the people on my paths in life and I am more of a gift, than a burden, to the Earth and those around me.

A challenge I find in discussing the depth of life we can lead when we have an active relationship with our dreams is that I may have a tendency of sounding aloof and over idealistic. If you met me you would see I am anything but aloof, though I am inspired with idealism. Practical idealism. Idealism in action is a do-able goal for any of us. I am *less* serious about life now, not more. I see humor in a good part of life, with magic and miracles happening every day.

My wish and hope for you is that you give your dreams a little attention and let the magic unfold in your life too. Bright Dreams!

THE POWER OF DREAMS

THE POWER OF DREAMS

About the Author

Susan Morgan is Native American (Abenaki and Huron) along with Scots Irish, and French roots. A certified dream teacher from The Robert Moss School of Active Dreaming, she is also a shamanic practitioner, healer and intuitive.

Susan is the former host of the critically acclaimed Mystic Dream Show which was produced by Emmy award winning Daniel Weaver and directed by Emmy nominated (11 times!) Lee Moore. She has an office in Exeter, New Hampshire but also travels all over, leading workshops and classes related to dreamwork. In addition to group work, Susan works privately.

Other books by Susan are (soon to be published): *The Inspired Dream Card Book*, along with *The Inspired Dream Card* deck to be released in 2011.

More info can be found about her on her website: MysticDreamCenter.com and facebook: Mystic Dream Center.

THE POWER OF DREAMS

Made in the USA
Charleston, SC
02 July 2011